It's Not Just PR

It's Not Just PR:
Public Relations in Society

W. Timothy Coombs
and Sherry J. Holladay

Blackwell
Publishing

© 2007 by W. Timothy Coombs and Sherry J. Holladay

BLACKWELL PUBLISHING
350 Main Street, Malden, MA 02148-5020, USA
9600 Garsington Road, Oxford OX4 2DQ, UK
550 Swanston Street, Carlton, Victoria 3053, Australia

The right of W. Timothy Coombs and Sherry J. Holladay to be identified as the Authors of this Work has been asserted in accordance with the UK Copyright, Designs, and Patents Act 1988.

First published 2007 by Blackwell Publishing Ltd

1   2007

Library of Congress Cataloging-in-Publication Data

Coombs, W. Timothy.
  It's not just PR : public relations in society / W. Timothy Coombs and Sherry J. Holladay.
      p. cm.
  Includes bibliographical references and index.
  ISBN-13: 978-1-4051-4405-6 (alk. paper)
  ISBN-10: 1-4051-4405-X (alk. paper)
  ISBN-13: 978-1-4051-4406-3 (pbk. : alk. paper)
  ISBN-10: 1-4051-4406-8 (pbk. : alk. paper) 1. Public relations–Social aspects. I. Holladay, Sherry J. II. Title.

  HM1221.C59 2007
  659.2–dc22

                     2006020245

A catalogue record for this title is available from the British Library.

Set in 10.5/12.5pt DanteMT
by SPi Publisher Services, Pondicherry, India
Printed and bound in Singapore
by COS Printers Pte Ltd

The publisher's policy is to use permanent paper from mills that operate a sustainable forestry policy, and which has been manufactured from pulp processed using acid-free and elementary chlorine-free practices. Furthermore, the publisher ensures that the text paper and cover board used have met acceptable environmental accreditation standards.

For further information on
Blackwell Publishing, visit our website:
www.blackwellpublishing.com

Contents

Introduction

We chose the title *It's Not Just PR: Public Relations in Society* to reflect the frustration experienced by many academicians and practitioners when the term "public relations" is misused by the media and misunderstood by the general population. For that term is probably among the most misunderstood and misapplied in our social milieu! Its colloquial use tends to be tainted with negative connotations as critics lament the substitution of "public relations" for facts, substance, or the "real story."

Public relations activities are often equated with spin, stonewalling, distortion, manipulation, or lying. The media tend to use the term "public relations" in ways that impugn the motives of the organization or person. When was the last time you heard public relations referred to in a way that did *not* imply something negative? People tend to regard anything labeled as "public relations" with great suspicion. Colloquial usage reflects a lack of understanding of the nature and practice of public relations. We have focused on the media's (mis)use of the term because most people do not have direct experience of the actual practice, and are dependent on the media in forming their ideas about it. The negative impression given may lead people to wonder if society would be better off entirely without public relations.

We invite readers to develop a more complex and complete understanding of the practice of public relations. *It's Not Just PR* should help readers understand why society benefits from the practice. Important to us in writing this book are the role of power in public relations and the use of public relations by non-corporate entities. These two topics are underdeveloped in the public relations literature and one of our motivations for writing this book. This book examines both the microlevel and

1

macrolevel (societal, global) outcomes of the practice of public relations. The microlevel examines what defines and constitutes public relations. We focus, as other public relations scholars do, on the relationship between organizations and their stakeholders, people who are affected by and can affect the organization. However, our discussion features the often neglected role of power in the relationship dynamic. The macrolevel focuses on how public relations can impact on society by influencing laws, values, and other actions. We address how the effects of public relations reach beyond national borders, and are now global.

We begin by discussing uses of the term "public relations" in the media and show how it tends to be greatly oversimplified and portrayed in a negative light. We also examine popular press treatments that typically equate public relations with corporate "publicity" and show how the focus on publicity limits our understanding of the range of public relations practices. We identify common criticisms of public relations with an eye to showing how they are often driven by concerns about power and one-way communication.

We then explore how academic conceptualizations of public relations differ from media portrayals. Academic definitions of public relations incorporate references to democratic elements by emphasizing the mutuality and interdependence of the relationships among organizations and stakeholders. Dialogue – the two-way exchange of messages and influence between organizations and stakeholders – is presented by some researchers as an effective and ethical way of cultivating and managing these relationships. Public relations offers a mechanism for people to be involved in the marketplace of ideas. We emphasize that, contrary to negative media portrayals, the process of public relations is not inherently corrupt. It is in fact designed to create mutual engagement and benefits to society. Our definition of public relations as the *management of mutually influential relationships within a web of stakeholder and organizational relationships* reflects a belief that public relations does have a strong persuasive component.

We address the way power resources and ethical concerns are implicated in the conducting of public relations. It is the role of public relations professionals to manage the interests of stakeholders and the interests of the organization. Their boundary-spanning role and ethical obligations place them in the position to listen to stakeholders and bring their concerns to the attention of management. The ethic of care is proposed as a useful framework for understanding the organization's obligations to stakeholders and their mutual interdependence.

People often think of corporations as very powerful compared to average citizens. Sources of power for stakeholders and organizations are discussed with an eye to demonstrating stakeholders' potential for influence. As suggested by stakeholder theory, stakeholders can develop power resources and influence corporations and the marketplace of ideas. However, in most cases the power advantage lies with the corporation. The interdependence between organizations and stakeholders is central to our appreciation of power dynamics and ethical practices in the relationships.

This book adopts a rather unusual, non-corporate perspective on the practice of public relations. Although we acknowledge its corporate connections, we eschew the corporate-centric standpoint in order to provide a more rounded view of public relations. We draw upon the literature on activist public relations and trace the roots of the practice to the social reform movements of the 1800s. We find, in analyzing historical events, that this sort of activity was going on long before the rise of modern corporations. We also discuss a wide range of contemporary examples of activist uses of public relations to influence public policy (the issues management model) and society, with positive and negative consequences.

At a macrolevel, we examine the ways public relations has been used to shape society for the better and for worse. We look at both national-level and global-level public relations efforts, and address how they transcend national boundaries. Global public relations as a form of transnational activism and public diplomacy has been growing. Its expansion and effectiveness has been aided by the Internet. Critics of public relations claim it is a tool used to hide "bad behavior" by spinning information and distracting stakeholders. But today, even multinational corporations find it difficult to hide unseemly and illegal activities. Activists use the Internet and public relations practices to shine light into the darkest, most remote areas of corporate activities. Odds are you have never been to a sweatshop in southeast Asia but you have probably heard that Nike and other apparel manufacturers have used them. Public relations can be utilized as a force for good in world.

We are not so naive as to believe that public relations is not used to pursue or to cover up courses of action that harm stakeholders and society. The Enron scandal was made possible through aggressive and deceptive media and investor relations. We will discuss other negative examples of public relations throughout this book. Public relations is not all-powerful, exclusively corporate, or always harmful to stakeholders and society. Nor is it only used by activists and non-profits to benefit stakeholders and society. The reality is that public relations is a complex mix of all these factors and more. Our goal is to complicate your thinking about public relations by peering behind the misuses of the term to examine its role in society. In the end, we hope this book demonstrates how public relations does have a place in and can be useful to society.

1

Does Society Need Public Relations?

Conceptualizations of what constitutes public relations cast a wide net and demonstrate a lack of consistency. And when something is labeled by the media as a "public relations" action, it seems to be with a negative, disparaging tone (e.g., "mere public relations," "PR spin," "PR hype," "PR rhetoric," or "a public relations stunt"). As described in the media, virtually anything that a corporation or its representatives does may be labeled as "public relations" and treated with suspicion. Activities as diverse as attempts to explain a negative financial report, launch a new product, encourage employees to volunteer in the community, and donate money to a charity, have all been identified as "public relations." What, then, is *not* public relations?

Critics of public relations tend to focus attention on what they call public relations efforts involved in defending the most obvious and egregious violations of the public trust: cover-ups (such as Enron, Tyco, and HealthSouth), CEO/CFO scandals, the spokesperson who deceives the public in order to defend the actions of the organization, and illegal dumping of toxic chemicals. Attempts to minimize or conceal these scandalous actions often are cast as "PR ploys" designed to deflect the negative impacts of questionable corporate actions including suspicious financial reports, management misbehavior, dubious environmental records, or human rights violations. Public relations becomes equated with stonewalling. Stonewalling is the attempt to hide information or delay its release. The public relations practitioner becomes a barrier to the truth, not the bringer of truth.

Scandals attract attention. Good deeds and the mundane are less likely to generate media exposure. What go unrecognized are the more commonplace and typical PR efforts that characterize the daily existence of organizations (e.g., employee communication, community relations, etc.). Examples include announcements about promotions, recognition of awards won by an organization, or efforts to support local charities or community groups. These more accurately characterize the PR efforts of most organizations. Very few PR practitioners are ever in the position of managing major scandals like those generated by Tyco, Enron, Health-South, or Martha Stewart. Public relations is the subject of heavy criticism in our culture. Upon learning of these criticisms, people are often left to ponder if society needs public relations. Without it, would society be better or worse off? Both professionals and academics have tried to defend the practice. Often the defense attributes to public relations very lofty pursuits, which seem rather unrealistic. By reviewing the good and the bad of public relations we can better appreciate its place in society.

The first half of the chapter examines the negative effects of public relations. We start by reviewing media portrayals. Most people learn about the practice of public relations through media coverage of the field and use of the term. Hence, the media help to construct people's perceptions. Public relations has some individual vocal critics as well. We examine the main critics and the reason for their disdain. As a corollary, some of the popular press books on public relations are surveyed. Public relations can be its own worst enemy by emphasizing the aspects most despised by its critics.

The second half of the chapter considers the utility of public relations to society. Practitioner and academic defenses of public relations are presented. The chapter ends by offering our conceptualization of public relations. We give a definition of public relations that highlights the role of communication, relationship management, and mutual influence between organizations and stakeholders. This provides the basis for understanding where public relations fits into the needs of society.

Media Use and the Term "PR"

Marion Jones was one of the brightest stars for the USA Track and Field team at the 2000 Sydney Olympics. She was the first woman to win five

Olympic medals in track and field. However, Jones's star quickly faded when she was swept into the vortex of the BALCO scandal. BALCO, a leading supplier of supplements to elite athletes, was discovered to have been supplying steroids and other banned performance-enhancing supplements. Victor Conte, the founder of BALCO, identified Marion Jones as one of the athletes he had helped to enhance in a series of late 2003 television interviews. Jones denied the accusations and filed a $25 million libel lawsuit against Conte. An article in *USA Today* quoted one source that referred to the lawsuit as "a public relations tactic" (Iwata and Patrick 2004). The media frequently equate public relations with over-the-top actions such as this excessive lawsuit, actions that are all style and no substance.

Although we frequently hear people refer to public relations, the practice of public relations is not well understood. The media may be at least in part to blame for the public's lack of understanding because they tend to use the term "public relations" inaccurately and to focus on some types of PR practice while ignoring others. It is important to consider seriously these portrayals of the uses of public relations and its professionals because they shape people's perceptions of what PR is, when it might be used, what PR professionals do, etc. The unfortunate part is that, as is shown by systematic research into media portrayals of public relations, comparing them with the reality, these portrayals are negative (for instance, they equate PR with lying) as well as quite limited. They fail to capture the full range of PR activities and focus mainly on publicity functions. Additionally, the media often label communications and actions as "mere PR" when they really are not what PR professionals would consider public relations. Overall, the media's use of the term "PR" seems fraught with negative connotations. Empirical research has established the extent of distortion there is in these portrayals. In 1988, Bishop discovered PR was equated with "publicity" in the newspaper coverage in a sample of three newspapers. Keenan (1996) found nearly half of the references to public relations in major network media coverage reflected the press agency model. Public relations was portrayed as nothing more than trying to generate media coverage. Julie Henderson (1998) examined the use of the term "public relations" in 100 popular press media articles. In about 5 percent of them the term PR was used accurately, in ways that would be acceptable to the Public Relations Society of America (PRSA), the professional association. This is problematic because the media are a key source of cues for building reputations when people have little interaction with an entity (Dowling 2002). Most people learn about public relations from the media, not from practitioners.

The problem of limited or inaccurate conceptions of public relations is compounded by the negative use of the term itself, as in the Marion Jones example, and by negative comments about PR. Henderson's (1998) research found that in only about 7 percent of the articles could the references to PR be considered "positive." Spicer (1993) found the majority (83 percent) of references to public relations in print media were negative.

Scrimger and Richards (2003) explored Canadian journalists' uses of metaphors of violent conflict to describe communication between organizations and the public. They examined articles where journalists used the term "public relations battle" or "public relations war." They found these phrases were invoked even though the reality of the situation often did not justify the use of inflammatory metaphors. In about one-half of the cases (55 percent), the terms were used in the first paragraph of the story. In all cases the choice of word was the journalists'; no sources were directly quoted as using either of the two phrases. Thus, their research demonstrates that journalists are prone to frame situations as "violent confrontations" (PR wars or battles) in spite of the fact that the participants do not describe their situations in this way. The media coverage offered a conflict frame even though there could be areas of consensus or agreement between the parties. These types of portrayals could lead the public to misperceive typical PR practices as involving fighting rather than collaboration. Research consistently demonstrates a negative portrayal of public relations and/or use of the term in the media. Media treatment of public relations is an indirect form of criticism. Others have been more direct in their disdain for public relations.

Criticisms of Public Relations

It is not difficult to locate critiques of the practice of public relations. Critics of public relations are numerous, vocal, and profess allegiance to a variety of disciplines. Critiques can be found in popular press books and in journalistic discussions of public relations. These sources are now reviewed to understand why public relations is considered by some to be a pariah in society.

Popular press attacks on public relations

Two popular press books stand out for casting a critical eye on the practice of public relations: *PR! A Social History of Spin* (1996) and *Toxic Sludge is Good for You!* (1995). Popular press books, in contrast to more academically oriented books, are aimed at a wide, general audience. It is noteworthy that there is little agreement in them on what constitutes public relations. These popular press books reflect an attitude that seemed particularly prevalent in the 1990s, a time that corresponds to the growth of corporate power. An underlying theme in both the books mentioned above is that large corporations are threatening and that public relations is one of the tentacles on this dangerous octopus.

Often popular press books present examples from the history of public relations, select dramatic illustrations to reveal its "unethical nature," and focus on how contemporary businesses (or governments) use PR to operate in order to pursue economic objectives at the expense of the public interest. The examples serve to represent the whole. Synecdoche is used as an argument. If part of what public relations does is bad, then everything public relations does is bad. A part comes to represent the whole.

Stuart Ewen's *PR! A Social History of Spin*, recounts the development of the practice of public relations by focusing on the commonly recognized pioneers of public relations, Edward Bernays (the "father of public relations") and Ivy Lee, and identifies scholars who influenced their thinking (e.g., Walter Lippmann, Gustave Le Bon). He also contextualized various public relations efforts conducted by private industry and government within various historical, economic, social, and corporate periods. Ewen writes that his book focuses on "the social and historical roots that would explain the boundless role of public relations in our world" (1996: 3). Interestingly, Ewen does not define a key word in his book's title, "spin" (nor does it appear in the index), perhaps because he assumes the savvy reader will assume that PR and spin are synonymous. (From the title alone, how is the prospective reader supposed to know that this is a book about public relations?)

Near the end of the book Ewen writes that public relations is designed to "circumvent critical thinking" and is "rarely intended to inform the population about the intricacies of an issue" (p. 412). He expresses concern over the fact that the techniques used have become increasingly "sophisticated" and "pervasive" (p. 409). A theme of this work is that PR poses a real threat to democracy because it undermines open, public discourse. Powerful corporations can hire skilled PR professionals and gain access to the media in order to advocate their policies and points of view; they thus exercise enormous influence, which the average person cannot match. He suggests that the general public is untrained and ill-informed in sophisticated PR methods, and not equipped to assess PR output.

In the final section of his book he advocates education in media literacy in order to equip citizens with the analytical tools needed to critically analyze media messages and images; this education should begin in primary grades. We believe that media literacy is a laudable goal, and people should be discriminating consumers of mediated messages. However, public relations is not the sole force responsible for its need. Ewen's book reflects a distrust of corporations: people must be wary of the deceptions enacted by corporations. And, as he says, public relations is a perfect mechanism for corporate deception.

John Stauber and Sheldon Rampton's *Toxic Sludge is Good for You! Lies, Damn Lies and the Public Relations Industry*, offers a highly critical view of PR which focuses on how it is used to deceive the public. Their goal is to enlighten the masses: "We want the public at large to recognize the skilled propagandists of industry and government who are affecting public opinion and determining public policies, while remaining (they hope) out of public view" (p. 16). They argue that the democratic process has been railroaded through the use of PR techniques. When we think corporations are doing something that is socially responsible or for the good of the public, we had better look more closely because we are merely being fooled. We should remain suspicious and scrutinize their PR actions to unmask what corporations gain from what seem to be noble acts.

The book is comprised of interesting, lively-written case studies designed to reveal PR's role in influencing public opinion and policy. Examples range from the tobacco industry's attempt to get women to smoke to phony grassroots movements (astroturf) to McDonald's partnering with Environmental Defense Fund, from the Environmental Protection Agency's involvement in getting communities to accept sludge farming to Hill and Knowlton's role in securing US citizens' support for the Persian Gulf War, and to Burson-Marsteller's part in securing support for NAFTA. Again, PR is presented as an all-powerful tool used by powerful interests (corporations, governments) to gain and maintain their power.

A recurring criticism in *Toxic Sludge is Good for You!* is that PR efforts are not easily recognized as such, which makes PR even more insidious and powerful. Advertising (usually) can be recognized as advertising and is commonly understood to represent something that a corporation has paid for and therefore invites critical examination. However, they argue, PR practices commonly include the coopting of journalists who, owing to financial and personnel cuts in their news organizations, have become dependent on PR practitioners for pitches for news stories, use of video news releases, and basic access to information in order to meet deadlines. This results in journalists producing news stories that actually benefit corporations rather than the public (meeting the public's "need to know"). What we think is "news" (because it appears in a newspaper or other media outlet) is really a pitch for corporate interests.

Stauber and Rampton also question the motives of organizations that partner with activist groups in efforts to appear socially responsible. While we might think that working with such groups is a sign of concern for the activists' issues, the corporations are the ones that actually benefit from the alliances. The authors claim that these alliances are used to benefit corporate interests and prevent the groups from interfering with business operations. By "coopting" the activists, corporations are able to gather information from the groups and "know the enemy." These alliances are designed to improve the image of the corporation and allow them to continue business as usual without truly addressing the contentious issues.

At times the authors seem ambivalent about the specific techniques and uses of public relations:

> The PR professionals who work to manage our opinions and emotions are not doing this because they are evil, but because PR is a financially rewarding business. From their viewpoint they are simply providing a service to their paying customers. If PR poses a threat to democratic

values, it is ultimately a manifestation of the deeper contradiction in corporate America – the gap between our dream of a governance "by the people, for the people" and the reality of a society deeply divided by unequal access to wealth and power (p. 203).

In contrast, they later write,

Many PR practitioners *are* engaged in promotional and publicity campaigns for clinics, schools and deserving charities that benefit the public. The techniques of public relations are not all inherently bad. Everyone at some time uses their skills of persuasion to communicate ideas, to sell products, promote a point of view, or "schmooze" socially. But positive uses of PR do not in any way mitigate the undemocratic power of the multi-billion dollar PR industry to manipulate and propagandize on behalf of wealthy special interests, dominating debate, discussion and decision (p. 205).

However, they do note that

Citizens and individual PR practitioners can use ethical public relations techniques to right social wrongs, clean up the environment, promote minority rights, protect working people and make their communities better. But we consider it an illusion to imagine that PR is a "neutral" technology that can simply be adopted uncritically to achieve socially responsible ends (pp. 205–6).

This last sentence seems to endorse the idea that the practice of PR is inherently corrupt.

While Stauber and Rampton admit they do not offer a "magic solution" to the problem posed by PR in society, they hope that their book will help people to "first, learn to recognize the influence of PR in your life; second, seek out alternative sources of information; third, become personally involved in local efforts to directly address important issues at the community level" (p. 204).

A film version of the book is available: *Toxic Sludge is Good for You: The Public Relations Industry Unspun*. Here is the creator's description of the film:

While advertising is the visible component of the corporate system, perhaps even more important and pervasive is its invisible partner, the public relations industry. This video illuminates this hidden sphere of our culture and examines the way in which the management of "the public mind" has become central to how our democracy is controlled by political and economic elites. *Toxic Sludge Is Good For You* illustrates how much of what we think of as independent, unbiased news and information has its origins in the boardrooms of the public relations companies.

Using interviews, the film repeats the primary points of the book. There also are interviews with former public relations professionals. These repentant individuals reveal the manipulative secrets of their trade. The focus remains on people not realizing that public relations helps to create the news through publicity efforts and how willing media representatives can be co-opted. Once more there is an underlying theme of the dangerous corporation. When non-corporate entities use public relations it is acceptable, but those corporations are sinister.

Stauber and Rampton are active in *PR Watch*, a quarterly publication from the Center for Media and Democracy that focuses on revealing the "dark side" of public relations. It bills itself as specializing in "blowing the lid off of the multi-billion dollar propaganda-for-hire industry" (*PR Watch*, 2005). The idea is that the newsletter, available free of charge online, reveals to people how public relations manipulates the news. By understanding the process, people will have a better chance of resisting it.

But perhaps the most vociferous critics can be found among the ranks of journalists. It is somewhat ironic that many historians trace the roots of modern public relations back to the actions of (former) journalists whose skills were purchased to benefit the interests of corporations. These journalists are described as leaving their positions with newspapers to assist corporations in appeasing the public. Corporations perceived that journalists possessed the skills needed to promote their organizations. Journalists' technical competence in writing press releases was coveted by corporations keen to defend themselves against public criticism of their business practices. Robber barons, the early US industrialists, were among the first to "corrupt" journalists. This was a major shift from the "Public be damned" attitude expressed by railroad tycoon William Vanderbilt and seemingly embraced by his brethren. The practice of "working for" a particular client and representing partisan interests may not sit well with journalists who embrace the journalistic ideal of the objective crusader and protector of the public trust. The image of the "hired gun" of the corporation contrasts starkly with the idealized image of the unbiased journalist.

Criticism of public relations is nothing new. In fact, criticism erupted as soon as modern public relations began to be practiced by corporations in the late 1800s and early 1900s. It is noteworthy that the early criticisms sound remarkably similar to current criticisms. There has always been a fear that public relations could be used to hide unwelcome information and might subvert the true reporting of news.

Of course, critics note it is rather ironic that PR should be so frequently misunderstood and accused of having an "image problem" when one component of their role is to manage information, public opinion, and corporate images. Critics seem to delight in pointing out the inability of PR to manage its own reputation. The implication is that if the "image masters" cannot successfully manage PR's image, the critics must be right! The practice of public relations must be so truly reprehensible that even the "spinmeisters" cannot salvage it. Critics interpret the inability of PR to elevate its reputation as further evidence of its inherent evil.

So what, exactly, drives the disparagement of the practice of PR? The following section outlines common themes expressed in critiques of public relations. This is followed by a few specific examples of what critical, popular press books have said about public relations practices.

Common themes in critiques of public relations

1. *Public relations has kept the public ignorant about what "really" goes on in public relations.*

The critical books are written and promoted as "exposés" on the PR industry. They promise to reveal behind-the-scenes machinations that will shock and sicken us and expose PR practitioners as the snake oil sales-people of our time. The public is portrayed as "duped" through the machinations of PR professionals who use sophisticated techniques to "spin" the truth. The public does not recognize PR efforts as being sponsored by and serving the interests of corporations or governments. The public is unaware of the nature and extent of PR and would be outraged "if only they knew." PR efforts are assumed to present lies, or at least distortions, of the truth.

2. *Public relations cannot escape its wicked roots.*

Early influences on the practice of public relations included writings on psychology and persuasion. The origins of public relations can be traced back to early writings concerning human behavior and the manipulation of public opinion and behavior. Early academic work on the nature and role of persuasion portrayed humans as easily malleable, given the use of the right techniques. The problem is that many of these writings seemed to privilege the "elite" (wealthy, well educated), suggesting that the less educated could and should be influenced by those who knew what was best for them. Within the context of contemporary society, the paternalistic attitudes expressed in many of these works seem exploitive and do not fully acknowledge the plethora of ethical concerns implicated in molding behavior.

Critics often point to the seminal influences, noting how this line of thinking corrupted early practitioners, and suggest that the origins continue to influence current practice. Public relations is tainted by the early ideas that underlie its practice. After all, Joseph Goebbels, mastermind of Nazi propaganda, claimed to be guided by a book entitled *Propaganda*, authored by Edward Bernays, the "father of public relations."

3. *PR is to blame for the inordinate amount of power that corporations (and other groups, governments, lobbying groups, etc.) can exercise.*

These criticisms focus on how public relations has been used to further the interests of these groups. Public relations efforts have been very successful in securing power for them. Corporations and governments are too powerful and public relations tactics are to blame. Corporations have become bullies. PR is what allows organizations to operate as they please, without interference from those who would question their practices. PR has duped the public into accepting this state of affairs.

These criticisms seem to ignore how the economic conditions and government policies have led to the development of corporate power. What they need to attack is the power of corporations to operate in the way that they do (what laws have made that possible), not the means used to get them to the point where they can exercise that power.

4.   *Public relations services are available to (or work for) those with "deep pockets" and this undermines the democratic process.*

Corporations use their seemingly unlimited economic resources to fight for their own interests at the expense of the well-being of the general citizenry and democracy itself. As described in no. 3, corporations are seen as too powerful. The once-revered, democratic, public debate of ideas is a myth in a world where public relations can sway public sentiment. This suggests that PR itself is undemocratic: It can be used in undemocratic ways for undemocratic ends.

While individuals and groups representing divergent interests can use PR techniques, the financial capabilities of corporations (or governments) far outweigh what is available to the individuals. Access to public relations is undemocratic, and this makes democracy impossible. The idea of the democratic process in today's society is a sham owing to the power of public relations to work for the interests of corporations.

5.   *Public relations' power can be curtailed (and democracy restored) if the public is educated in how to resist public relations.*

The public needs to be informed and educated about public relations in order to resist its influence. People must be vigilant in separating public relations ploys from the "truth." The public can protect itself from the influence of public relations and reclaim democracy. When corporations win through PR efforts, the "public good" loses.

6.   *Public relations is only publicity.*

The critics of public relations treat it as publicity; they see the function of PR as influencing media content. That is indeed part of public relations, but often a small part. The latter part of this chapter will present more rounded and informed definitions of public relations. For example, in 2005 MTV featured a look at what they called "the PR industry" entitled *PoweRGirls*. This program showed young females working entirely in publicity, representing clients and being responsible for orchestrating glamorous club openings, CD promotions, and fashion show attendance. Here is a description of one episode: "Ali has one week to prepare a new Sony band, the Valli Girls, for their red carpet debut at the Teen People party. Teaching the Valli Girls to pose, walk and answer journalists' questions seems to be going well . . . until one of the Valli Girls makes a gross, inappropriate comment during an interview with an *Elle Girl* reporter" (Episode 106 summary, 2005). The *Boston Globe* described the show as "a chaotic look at the world of PR flacks and how a team of Manhattan chippies gets press for rich customers" (Gilbert 2005). We believe that this is probably the most prominent glimpse into the world of public relations – and all that is shown is a publicity-only agency, staffed by attractive young women, that opens clubs and promotes records. What value is being added to society with this?

In conclusion, these six common criticisms of public relations clearly point to the conclusion that not only does society *not* need public relations, it would be better off without it. Public relations subverts and weakens the news media. Moreover, corporations use public relations to deceive and to harm stakeholders.

Popular Press Books Describing the Importance of Public Relations

At the other end of the spectrum are popular press books describing the potential of public relations to impact positively on contemporary organizations. In contrast to the popular books with a negative account of public relations, these are targeted at professionals in any business. There are far more books promoting the value of public relations than there are criticizing it. Their concern is with how practitioners are positioning or describing their own field. The following examples are from more positive portrayals of public relations and focus on descriptions of it and recommended use of PR to benefit organizations. We selected two representative popular press pro-public relations books on the basis of sales figures and citations by others.

The book *The Fall of Advertising and the Rise of PR* (Ries and Ries 2002) focuses on the growing importance of PR and brand-building for contemporary organizations. The authors conceptualize PR in terms of publicity. Although the title seems to portend the death of advertising, Ries and Ries contend that the role of advertising has been misunderstood and misused by corporations. At the same time, the potential role of PR has been overlooked because of an overemphasis on advertising. The authors propose that elevating the role of PR in brand-building is a good business practice that will benefit corporations.

Ries and Ries begin with the thesis that marketing is the most important function of a corporation, and PR-oriented marketing should be emphasized over advertising. They assert that the significance of advertising has been greatly overrated. The public is inundated with advertisements and is skeptical of these paid-for messages. Moreover, too much emphasis on "creativity in advertising" has actually interfered with the impact of advertising. This does not mean we should sound the death knell: advertising is not dead. However, it should play a secondary role to PR because PR involves a strategy for building brands while advertising offers no long-term strategy. PR should be used for brand-building, the central function of marketing, while advertising should be used for brand maintenance, representing a continuation of PR. Advertising, they argue, cannot build (or re-build) a brand. Advertising cannot change minds. Advertising can only provide consumers with "reminders" about established brands. It can only reinforce a perception, not create or change a perception the way that PR can. PR must be the central focus of marketing.

Reis and Reis focus on PR narrowly defined as generating media coverage that is designed to garner publicity and build brands. They ignore other PR functions that do not relate to publicity and brand-building. For example, they discuss the importance of having a celebrity spokesperson, such as the CEO (like Martha Stewart, Richard Branson, the late Dave Thomas, or Wolfgang Puck), to be the face and voice of the brand. Additionally, they note the need to be the "first" in a category (or create the new category for the product) because the media want to report on what is new or what is first. Also, they claim it is important to encourage the media to feature the credentials of the company by mentioning their leadership in the category. For instance, Volvo is perceived as the automobile industry leader in safety. Focusing on the value of publicity in generating interest, they discuss the importance of "free media" and word of mouth endorsements.

However, the authors note that while using advertising permits complete control over the message, using PR means accepting a lack of control. The authors are equating public relations with publicity, and publicity is a medium not easily controlled. The public relations professional sends out a news release, pitch letter, or video news release (VNR). But the media representative decides or controls if the information is used (placement), how the information will be used (content), and when the information will be used (timing). With an advertisement or a web site, the public relations professional controls placement, content, and timing. The trade-off, for losing some of that control, is that media attention gained through PR techniques is perceived as more trustworthy and is less expensive than advertising.

The book documents many examples of how PR has been used successfully to build brands in different industries, including toy brands, alcohol brands, drug brands, transportation brands, and high-tech brands. Readers no doubt recognize the examples they provide.

It is interesting to note that, in the postscript section, the authors lament the fact that definitions of PR itself do not mention brand-building as a PR function. They accuse PR, including its professional association (PRSA, the Public Relations Society of America), of being ineffective at brand-building by not exploiting "the core objective of your speciality" (p. 280). In contrast, they note that the AAF (American Advertising Federation) portrays itself with the slogan "Advertising. The way great brands get to be great brands." Reis and Reis argue that other PR functions are meaningless if the company cannot succeed at building strong brands.

Overall, this book endorses the role of public relations in garnering media attention and building brands. Their treatment of PR functions is rather limited and focuses on publicity-generating functions of PR strategy. They also limit their focus to brand-building and re-building.

Another popular press book, *Full Frontal PR: Building Buzz about Your Business, Your Product, or You* (Laermer 2004), discusses the importance of creating "buzz" (defined as getting people and the media to speak enthusiastically about your brand) through techniques that "blur the lines between traditional PR and marketing" (p. 4). Richard Laermer argues the two should work together to present and strengthen a unified image. This book focuses on media relations, working with the media in order to gain exposure and publicity. He argues, "The aim of public relations is to distribute information to the masses" (p. 30). Like Reis and Reis, he believes that building awareness and building brands should be the key PR function.

Laermer discusses the importance of making news and spreading information about new products or services through media stories and word of mouth rather than traditional forms of advertising. Like Reis and Reis, Laermer notes that advertising is regarded with suspicion and is ignored by the public. Because news is perceived to be more credible than advertising, people will pay more attention to news. "Free press actually validates your company or product in readers' minds" (p. xiii). He contends that word of mouth publicity offers the best exposure because it also seems credible. Once more, public relations is equated with publicity.

Laermer offers advice on how to work with the media to garner publicity. He describes the relationship between public relations practitioners and journalists as a potential "win-win" relationship. Because journalists are stressed and working under tight deadlines, they are eager to pursue good story ideas which PR practitioners can supply. "They need you as much as you need them" (p. xiv). Laermer offers advice on how to sell story ideas to journalists by focusing on news values that are important to journalists: proposing a local angle on the story, connecting to other stories, using celebrities, and so forth.

The idea is that PR should use publicity techniques to generate interest and enthusiasm that makes products or services hot and desirable. He notes that often this does not happen overnight and typically requires a sustained campaign. The book offers numerous examples to demonstrate the power of "buzz."

In sum, what is noteworthy about these popular press books offering positive depictions of PR is their focus on the publicity-generating function of PR to the exclusion of other PR functions. They focus on the importance of attracting media attention, how to work with the media in order to "get your story out there," and how this media attention will help establish brands. They also share a recognition of the limits of advertising in launching new brands, noting that the public is skeptical of traditional advertising and is more easily influenced by "free" media attention. In essence, the pro-public relations books feed into their critics' concerns. Public relations is still basically publicity. The pro-public relations books are pro-corporation; thus publicity is now considered a good thing because it helps clients. There is no real defense of public relations to be found in these books. But public relations is considered useful to society because it does help business.

Professional and Academic Defense of Public Relations

The defense of public relations as contributing to society has fallen to the profession and academics interested in public relations. Key to the defense is the definition. Publicity is but only one tool used by practitioners, not the entire field. Again the issue is synecdoche. Publicity, a part, comes to represent the whole of public relations.

The profession: The Public Relations Society of America (PRSA)

Naturally, those who practice public relations argue that popular press books and other media that criticize PR are unfair in their one-sided presentations of the reality of the practice. They take issue with the idea that PR requires lying, manipulation, "hype," and distortions of the truth.

PRSA is the largest professional organization of public relations practitioners in the United States. It notes that the field began as publicity but has evolved far beyond its roots. The emphasis is on the use of research, planning, communication, and evaluation. The official PRSA definition is "Public relations helps an organization and its publics adapt mutually to each other" (About Public Relations, 2005). The concern is not just to represent the organization through publicity. It is to work with publics so that they derive benefits from the relationship with the organization. If we accept that public relations benefits its publics, we can accept that it is useful to society.

Academics defend the practice

Scholars who are sensitive to criticisms of public relations have grappled with the condemnations of the field. There is no shortage of debate among academicians and practitioners interested in these issues. They address issues such as: what is the purpose of public relations? What is the role of the public relations practitioner? What is the place of public relations in contemporary society? How should we conceive of the public(s) (the stakeholders)? What constitutes ethical (and unethical) practices in public relations? These issues have spurred debate throughout the evolution of public relations and no doubt will continue to inspire discussion in the future.

Contemporary definitions of public relations describe PR practices as respectful of and contingent upon the public's interests. For example, in one of the most widely cited definitions of public relations, Cutlip et al. (1994) assert "Public relations is the management function that establishes and maintains mutually beneficial relationships between an organization and the public on whom its success or failure depends" (p. 2). Note how it resonates with PRSA's notions of adapting mutually. The idea is that public relations activities facilitate the development and maintenance of the relationship between an organization and the public.

A key component of this definition is "mutually beneficial relationships" (MBRs). As Robert Heath (2001) observed, the focus is on relationship building "to reduce the costs of conflict" (p. 2). Public relations "encourages publics to support rather than contest or oppose their efforts" (Heath, 2001, p. 8). The emphasis on relationships between organizations and the public reflects the goal of achieving dialogue – as opposed to monologue – with the public. The idea of dialogue suggests give and take – mutual influence – while monologue is a one-way form of communication and influence. The term "mutually beneficial relationships" is designed to reflect the idea of shared power between organizations and stakeholders.

However, Heath (2005) thinks that this definition may very well reflect an ideal situation rather than reality. The definition represents a normative model, one that may be highly desirable but difficult to achieve in practice (p. 552). He notes that while it certainly is desirable to be in a situation where the organizations and the stakeholders benefit because of their relationships, this may be more of a platitude and "may mask the darker intent and ability of the focal organization to persuasively promote the conclusion that the relationship is more mutually beneficial than it truly is" (p. 552).

Another component within that definition of public relations, "upon whom its success or failure depends," implicates power. It seems to suggest that these relationships with stakeholders are important because they can affect the operations of the organization and ultimately its success or failure. This gets back to the idea that not all relationships with stakeholder groups are created equal. Some stakeholder groups, those that can dramatically affect organizational success, may be more highly valued than others. "We will work to meet the expectations of society and establish MBRs as long as it does not threaten the sustainability of the corporation." Is this really unreasonable? Most organizations – with the exceptions of certain organizations developed for the purpose of serving society – exist as money-making enterprises. No one is naive enough to question that premise. However, that does not preclude corporations *working with* stakeholders to negotiate what is reasonable for operations. The result is probably more likely to be a compromise, with organizations giving less than the public expectations would demand.

Public Relations and the Marketplace of Ideas

A tenet of our democratic society is the free exchange of ideas. The metaphor of the "marketplace of ideas" is often used to describe the process. Everyone has a chance to voice his or her ideas. In fact, the First Amendment to the US Constitution is premised on the right of people to be heard, not for someone to speak. The ideas compete in the market-place and the winner is the one accepted by the most people. Public relations is a way for people to be involved in the marketplace of ideas. It allows them to share and to understand ideas before making a choice (Heath 2005).

People need to have their ideas heard. Public relations is a means of making ideas audible. Just as all defendants have the right to an attorney, all people have a right to have someone help them be heard. We realize that law is often held in low public esteem but it is an essential part of our society. Public relations can be a communication mechanism for binding society together through the facilitation of the marketplace of ideas, and so be valuable and essential to society. As with the law, public relations can be twisted and misused. However, that does not diminish its overall contribution to society.

However, in the criticisms of PR there is an element of idealism; this is a concern about power. One argument against PR practices is that they reflect unequal power relationships among senders and receivers, between PR practitioners and "the public"; it is through PR, it is said, that powerful, wealthy, corporations present their interests and impose their will on the unsuspecting public. The notion of power will therefore be a recurring theme throughout this book.

Re-focusing Public Relations

As this chapter suggests, public relations has no single, accepted definition for the field. But what has come to dominate recent definitions is the idea of mutually beneficial relationships. This reflects an emphasis on the outcome of PR activity, and an often idealistic one at that. In this book we propose a definition of public relations that is rooted in public relations' fundamental terrain and that acknowledges that public relations is conducted for some actor. Organizations (profit, nonprofit, and governmental) are the primary actors utilizing public relations. Hence, we shall start constructing public relations' terrain on the organization. Organizations exist within and because of a complex web of mutually influential relationships with stakeholders. In the classical sense, *stakeholders are any group that can affect or be affected by the actions of an organization* (Freeman 1984; Bryson 2004). The *stake* is the connection between the group or individual and the organization. Stakes can be tangible (e.g., financial) or intangible (e.g., support) (Heath 1997). Stakeholders can reside inside or outside of an organization (Ulmer et al. 2005). Typical stakeholders include employees, shareholders, customers, government entities, suppliers, communities, news media, and activists (Agle et al. 1999). *Publics* are "identifiable groups, either inside or outside the organization, whose opinion on issues can affect the success of the organization" (Heath and Coombs 2006: 9). Publics are collectives that form in response to some issue/problematic situation (Grunig and Hunt 1984; Vasquez and Taylor 2001). Publics have an issue-oriented stake in an organization. While overlapping, "stakeholder" tends to be the broader of the two terms. Hence, we favor the use of that term over "publics." Moreover, the stakeholder perspective takes more account of the often conflicting demands that various groups place on an organization (Bryson 2004; Ulmer et al. 2005). The notion of multiple, conflicting groups is a very realistic representation of the milieu for public relations.

Stakes can be premised on material and social capital. Material capital includes money, equipment, supplies, and products. Material resources include customers buying products, stakeholders investing money, corporations paying taxes, and employees earning wages. Social capital can be defined as the "resources embedded in a social structure which are accessed and/or mobilized in purposive actions " (Lin 1999: 35). Social capital is built through social networks or with those whom people know. Organizations and stakeholders form a type of social network. The connections with others rely on a degree of trust and a norm of reciprocity between the parties. One party can draw upon the other for assistance, which might be in the form of information, contacts, or influence. Social capital is a function of social networks and the benefits derived from those networks. These connections should build trust and serve to facilitate cooperation and coordination between members of the network (Putnam 2000; Saxton and Benson 2005). In one way, social capital is a reservoir of good will to be accessed when needed. Customers making positive word-of-mouth comments, employees praising the organization, and communities supporting re-zoning efforts are examples of social capital.

Organizations should recognize the value of the stakeholders. Research has established that a failure to attend to the needs of stakeholders is a "flaw" that often leads to poor performance (Bryson 2004). On occasion, stakeholders can influence organizational performance. The interconnection between organizations and stakeholders is therefore the basis for mutual influence. Influence is a matter of power or the ability to get an actor to do something it might not otherwise do. While each side can influence the relationship and also resist the influence, they do not, typically, do so to an equal extent. In most cases the organization has greater influence and the ability to resist; but the stakeholder does have some influence and some ability to resist. Resistance is a matter of having options for acting other than predicted.

In order to perform well, an organization needs a sense of order to prevail in its network of stakeholders. Because conflict among them can impede performance, a goal of public relations is to maintain harmony. But one way stakeholders can exercise power is to disrupt the harmony by some form of agitation. Any actor in the network can use PR activity to spread unrest. Conflict is a mechanism stakeholders have to remind organizations of their influence and to consider their needs. The squeaky wheel does get the oil. Indeed, organizations often benefit from this conflict by gaining insight into stakeholder needs, and this provides an impetus for beneficial change. Moreover, there may be times when organizations want to agitate stakeholders and get them involved in some external cause. Efforts to defeat or to support legislative proposals might involve organizations inciting their stakeholders to action. Taking all this into account, we define public relations (as mentioned in the Introduction) as *the management of mutually influential relationships within a web of stakeholder and organizational relationships.* Public relations, like power, is enacted and managed through communication. We include "management" in our definition because we assume that relationships do not merely happen by themselves. Just as interpersonal relationships require deliberate attention and communication skills to be maintained, intensified, or dissolved, relationships between organizations and stakeholders require management. The inclusion of "web of relationships" in this definition acknowledges there are multiple relationships that must be considered, including those that exist among various stakeholders and other organizations. The ties that bind are complex indeed!

Our definition of public relations is not revolutionary because it is consistent with prevailing views in the field. Hazleton and Kennan (2000) have used Bourdieu's (1985) work to link social capital to public relations. According to Bourdieu, social capital is "the aggregate of the actual or potential resources which are linked to possession of a durable network of more or less institutionalized relationships of mutual acquaintance or recognition" (p. 248). Organizations need to have stores of social capital and the ability to access those resources. Public relations can aid an organization in developing and accessing social capital. In turn, social capital reduces transaction costs for the organization. It reduces the financial costs of "doing business" (Hazleton and Kennan 2000). Grunig and Repper (1992) also noted that public relations can improve organizational effectiveness by building relationships with stakeholders and thereby facilitating the achievement of the organization's mission.

Grunig and Hon (1999) identified control mutuality as one of the key dimensions for evaluating relationships in public relations. Control mutuality means that both the organization and the stakeholder have some amount of control over the relationship. They also observed that power imbalances do occur in the organization-stakeholder relationship. Treating public relations as managing mutually influential relationships is consistent with current thinking in public relations. However, by re-focusing on *mutually influential relationships* we want to emphasize the role of interlacing stakeholder relationships and the centrality of *power* in those relationships.

Conclusion

In his book *Walden Two*, B. F. Skinner paints a picture of a utopian society. This society is built on his principles of operant conditioning. What is interesting is that even in a utopian society, Skinner recognized the need for public relations. Moving from fiction to reality, public relations is an inevitable and essential part of society, much like law. Ideas must be heard and public relations is a valuable megaphone for ideas. We may not like all the ideas we hear and some can abuse the megaphone for despicable ends, but society is poorer if that megaphone does not exist. Public relations is not without its problems. The greatest problem for public relations is the issue of power. Power is a serious concern that public relations has skated round with the skill of a professional dancer. Chapter 2 addresses the power issue more fully and explores the implications of power for both public relations and society.

2

Ethical Implications of Public Relations

At its heart, public relations is public communication. Public communicators always have had special ethical responsibilities and challenges because of the potential they have for abusing their positions (Starck and Kruckeberg 2003). This chapter reviews the ethical concern that public communicators have when establishing the lineage of today's public relations professionals. They have a boundary-spanning role in that they have to understand the needs of their client (the organization) as well as those of society as a whole. Even if inclined to privilege the interests of society, they are under pressure to favor their client. So the issue of power is examined in relation to the choices they make.

In Chapter 1 we discussed common critiques of public relations and focused on how popular press books and media often criticize the practice of public relations. Most criticisms of PR focus on its potential to influence public opinion, arguing that PR supports particular interests, for whose benefit the truth is often distorted. We noted how the publicity functions of PR tend to be overemphasized in discussions of the profession. We also discussed how inaccurate media depictions of PR practices may have a deleterious effect on people's perceptions of the profession. This chapter concentrates on public relations as a form of *public communication*. We will explore how public communication is associated with multiple, special responsibilities to society. These responsibilities stem from the need to practice ethical communication and the concomitant emphasis on two-way communication and dialogue in the public arena. Ethical responsibilities also extend to the treatment of clients because PR professionals are obligated to represent the interests of their clients. The concern for balancing the needs of society and the needs of clients produces a tension that may be difficult to manage. PR professionals may find it challenging to function as the "conscience of the organization" when the organization is their employer.

What is Public Communication?

The roots of the concern for public communication can be traced back through what is called "the rhetorical tradition." The rhetorical tradition is associated with a concern for public discourse, argument, and the character of the communicators. Early Greek and Roman rhetoricians such as Aristotle, Cicero, and Quintillian wrote about the importance of public discourse (public speaking) in the open exchange of ideas and extolled its role in creating a just, democratic society. They were especially concerned with the ethical responsibilities of public communicators. They endorsed the idea that public communicators should use sound reasoning, provide evidence, and be held accountable for their statements. They also noted that different message strategies could be used to achieve speakers' goals.

Early rhetoricians were especially sensitive to how the character of the communicator (credibility, goodwill toward others, morality, concern with ethics) figured in public communication. Although they noted that public discourse could be used by unscrupulous characters to pursue evil ends, the writers in the rhetorical tradition placed a premium on the use of ethical communication in public discourse. They saw the public arena as the place where differing ideas could be proposed, supported, and debated by citizens in order to determine which arguments should prevail. They valued public discussions because they believed this process enabled the most just ideas to emerge. Open, ethical public communication was seen as an integral part of the democratic process. These early scholars were endorsing what we now call the marketplace of ideas. People should hear all views on an issue in order to make informed decisions.

W. Timothy Coombs and Sherry J. Holladay

Ethical Responsibilities of PR as a Form of Public Communication

Although the early rhetoricians may seem far removed from today's modern society, their concerns about the power of public communication and the ethical obligations associated with public communication provide a strong legacy for American philosophy as well as offer implications for the practice of public relations. In theory and practice, we can think of ethics as standards for behavior that influence evaluations of what is right and wrong. Ethics are about values, and personal, organizational, and societal standards (Treadwell and Treadwell 2005). Textbooks on public relations include chapters on the ethical responsibilities of PR professionals and many academic programs require one or more classes in ethics as part of career preparation. In spite of the training in ethics, it is easy to see how PR professionals face many ethical dilemmas in the course of performing their roles as public communicators.

Public relations activities are performed within the context of a society whose members may (and should!) critically examine the activities with respect to their credibility, truthfulness, and intent. In the marketplace of ideas, we expect a variety of perspectives to compete for attention and endorsement by the public. We also expect these ideas to withstand careful scrutiny by a skeptical public. The knowledge that any public communication must be able to endure inspection should motivate PR professionals to consider seriously the ethical implications of their roles as public communicators and to exercise care when sending messages to the public. Shannon Bowen, in the "Ethics of public relations," writes, "The power to influence society means that public relations holds enormous responsibility to be ethical" (2005a: 294). The potential for public relations practitioners to shape public opinion necessarily puts pressure on them to consider, and practice, ethical communication. They should strive to protect the public interest.

While it is easy to see that ethics are implicated in message dissemination and influence attempts, we also should consider how ethics are associated with listening. PR professionals typically are portrayed as message senders and as engaging in one-way communication. We assume they are hired to place their client's message "out there" in the public arena. Critiques of public relations often assume this one-way view of communication. But this is only one side of the communication process. PR professionals must also listen. We should advocate *ethical listening* as well as speaking. Just as we expect the citizenry in a democratic society to listen to ideas in order to evaluate their merits and make informed decisions, PR professionals are obligated to listen to their stakeholders and consider their concerns. Stakeholders may be the ultimate judges of what constitutes ethical communication by the organization. The public may rightfully expect *dialogue* – a give and take of communication – with the organization. Dialogue requires listening. Listening represents the "two" in two-way communication while "one" is simply sending a message via one-way communication.

Ethical Perspectives

Thus far we have been discussing ethics in general. However, there are different ethical perspectives grounded in different assumptions. The merits of these perspectives can be compared, contrasted, and debated. We present two commonly referenced ethical perspectives and then propose that a third perspective best captures the ethical responsibilities implicated in how we have conceptualized the practice of public relations.

Two general perspectives on ethics include teleology and deontology. A *teleological* approach to ethics focuses on the *outcomes* of actions. A teleological ethical framework judges behavior according to its outcomes or consequences. You might violate the law (behave unethically) because it will result in a positive outcome. This can lead to the view that the "ends justify the means." A utilitarian teleological perspective suggests that outcomes or consequences of an action should be evaluated in terms of its effects. The preferred action should be the one that creates positive outcomes for the greatest number of people.

In contrast, the basis for the *deontological* ethical framework is a system of *rights, obligations, and duties*. This approach is dependent upon certain obligations between actors (e.g., contractual commitments) or between organizations and actors (e.g., the Equal Employment Opportunity Commission and workers). Laws, regulations, moral rules, and codes can be used as the standards for determining if behaviors are ethical. The codes of ethics for many professional associations can be viewed as reflecting this ethical sensibility. As we will see in a later section, the discussion of the codes of ethics for two professional associations affiliated with public relations reflects the deontological ethical framework.

A third perspective that has received limited attention in public relations is the *ethic of care*. The ethic of care is closely associated with the work of Carol Gilligan, a feminist writer who viewed *interdependence* as central to ethical behavior (Simola 2003). An ethic of care places the focus of ethics on "maintaining connections and nurturing the web of relationships" (p. 354). The recognition of the importance of the web of relationships fits well with our view of public relations as managing mutually influential relationships within a web of stakeholder and organizational relationships. The ethic of care's focus on interdependence, mutuality, and reciprocity mirrors our perspective on public relations.

An ethic of care fights the indifference found in other ethical systems. We have a responsibility to others to work to strengthen our relationships. This is possible through dialogue because it demonstrates a sense of responsibility to others. We cannot choose to ignore a relationship (with a stakeholder) simply because it is not that important to us. We must respect others and maintain connections (Simola 2003). This is consistent with recent writing on moral competence that stresses doing the "right thing." A key component of doing what is right is compassion or caring about others. An organization must align its values with its actions; if it says it cares it must show it cares (Lennick and Kiel 2005).

Corporate social responsibility offers an excellent illustration of the ethic of care. An organization can choose to address social and environmental concerns because it is compelled to do so by law or because it will help the organization achieve other goals. However, it can also choose to ignore social and environmental concerns because it is not mandated to address them or the stakeholder expressing concern has little power. An ethic of care argues that an organization should address social and environmental concerns because it will strengthen relationships with stakeholders by showing respect for their concerns.

We run into issues of impugning motives as we try to understand why an organization undertook an action. What we can evaluate are the actions. Are organizations taking actions that are beyond what is required by law and taking those actions before stakeholders have called for the actions? Acting beyond legal requirements and acting before being compelled to do so by stakeholder protests implies an ethic of care. We still can be skeptical that the organization is looking for some eventual gain from improving the relationship with stakeholders. True, organizations do increase social and material capital through relationships with stakeholders. The benefits are a natural outgrowth of the relationship network, regardless of the motive. Hence, we choose to consider the nature of the action because motives cannot be fully known. If an organization says it values care and reflects those values in its actions, we will consider it to be morally competent and reflecting the ethic of care.

Professional Associations and Ethics

The professional associations to which many PR practitioners belong endorse adherence to ethical standards that stem from the acknowledgment of the potential power of public communication to shape opinions as well as a concern for clients whose interests they serve. We offer a few excerpts from the Public Relations Society of America (PRSA) and International Association of Business Communicators (IABC) codes of ethics to illustrate the emphasis on both public communication and clients' interests. PRSA is geared specifically for PR professionals while the IABC claims a membership comprised of professionals from a wider range of occupations. The codes seem to reflect the deontological ethical perspective and its concomitant emphasis on obligations and duties to clients and the public. However, the concept of mutual adaptation is included in PRSA's definition of public relations; this suggests the relationship and mutuality aspects of the ethic of care.

The PRSA code of ethics (*PRSA Member Code of Ethics*, 2000) contains a section titled "Professional values." Under the "Advocacy" value, the code notes: "We serve the public interest by acting as responsible advocates for those we represent" (p. 7) and "We provide a voice in the marketplace of ideas, facts, and viewpoints to aid informed public debate" (p. 7). The "Honesty" value notes the concern with "accuracy and truth in advancing the interests of those we represent and in communicating with the public" (p. 7). The "Loyalty" value asserts "We are faithful to those we represent, while honoring our obligation to serve the public interest" (p. 8).

The PRSA "Code provisions" outlines core principles that should guide the goals and practices of PR. The core principle concerning the "Free flow of information" is: "Protecting and advancing the free flow of information is essential to serving the public interest and contributing to informed decision-making in a democratic society" (p. 9). Another core principle, one guiding the "Disclosure of information," is: "Open communication fosters informed decision-making in a democratic society" (p. 11). A core principle for "Enhancing the profession" is: "Public relations professionals work constantly to strengthen the public's trust in the profession" (p. 14). This includes the goal of building respect and credibility for the profession.

IABC is another professional organization to which PR professionals may belong, along with people from a wide variety of other professions. The Code of Ethics for Professional Communicators explains

> Because hundreds of thousands of business communicators worldwide engage in activities that affect the lives of millions of people, and because this power carries with it significant social responsibilities, the International Association of Business Communicators developed the Code of Ethics for Professional Communicators. (IABC code of ethics)

Like PRSA's code of ethics, IABC's code claims it members will be ethical in their communication and "engage in truthful, accurate and fair communication that facilitates respect and mutual understanding."

It is interesting to note the focus on the professional as the provider of information that aids the public's decision-making. Phrases like "disseminate accurate information" and foster "the free flow of essential information in accord with the public interest" are included. The IABC code notes that communication that contributes to "mutual understanding" should be encouraged. Although the role of listening may be implied, it is largely overlooked. Nowhere is listening explicitly referenced in either code. It seems logical that cultivating mutual understanding requires listening. But how should that happen in accordance with the codes? What does ethical listening "look like"?

Overall, the picture that emerges from these codes is consistent with the recognition of ethical responsibilities that derive from the power of public communication to influence society as a whole. Truthful, timely information that serves the public interest and facilitates informed decision-making is emphasized. However, the codes also note that professionals must simultaneously be concerned with serving the needs of clients. PRSA's code frequently references the importance of being faithful to "those we represent." The implication is that ethical communication entails representing client interests. After all, the profession could not exist without clients or employing organizations. So professionals should listen to their clients/organizations to determine how to meet their needs. But where is the parallel mandate for listening to stakeholders? The importance of ethical listening is implied but not explicitly stated. The code offers no specific guidelines for ethical listening.

The PR professional must walk a fine line in meeting the needs of both the client and the public. When is the line crossed between serving the public and serving the client? Undoubtedly professionals recognize some tension between the two. Although specific methods for resolving dilemmas involving possible conflicts between the public good and client needs are not provided, the codes seem to suggest that professionals should privilege the interests of society over those of clients by providing accurate and timely information that can be used for decision-making. But can they really serve two masters?

The Boundary-spanning Role of the PR Professional

It is clear that PR professionals may be placed "in the middle" when attempting to balance the needs of clients with the needs of society. PR professionals are in a rather unusual position as boundary-spanners. They take on this role when they connect the organization/client with society as a whole. In other words, while PR professionals are members of their organizations, they also have frequent and close contact with the public, which is composed of multiple stakeholder groups. The communications they craft for clients are introduced into the public forum. It is this communication with and to the public that necessitates a close consideration of ethical responsibilities in communication.

In this role of boundary-spanner we see the importance of the concept of mutually influential relationships in understanding public relations. Basic communication models recognize a distinction between one-way and two-way communication. As we previously discussed, one-way communication reflects the basic "sender to receiver model" (uni-directional model) where the speaker addresses an audience. Two-way communication implies an interaction between sender and receiver where the roles may switch. The receiver at least provides feedback to the sender about the message. Two-way communication involves both speaking and listening to stakeholders. The PR professional not only communicates to stakeholders, he or she attends to what stakeholders have to say with respect to organizational actions. Mutual influence arises from two-way communication.

Public relations theorists have tried to impose a second distinction on forms of two-way communication by drawing an additional distinction between asymmetrical and symmetrical models of two-way communication. Public relations scholar James Grunig (2001) popularized the distinction between two-way asymmetrical and two-way symmetrical models of public relations. The asymmetrical model focuses on the persuasive attempts of the organization to influence a stakeholder. The organization/client is trying to change the attitudes or behaviors of the stakeholder. However, because it is two-way communication, listening by the organization is viewed as a precursor to persuasion. The model assumes that the organization listens in order to persuade. But it also assumes that the organization does not adapt to what it hears from the stakeholder (Grunig and Hunt 1984).

The asymmetrical model neglects to consider that the organization can be changed by the information it collects from the stakeholder in the two-way communication. For instance, when McDonald's collected information about recycling Styrofoam in preparation for a new campaign to enhance its reputation, it discovered that customers could not accept that Styrofoam could be recycled. As a result, McDonald's scrapped the recycling plans in favor of a plan to replace Styrofoam sandwich containers with paper and cardboard wrappers. This example demonstrates that organizations using a two-way asymmetrical model can be changed by what they hear from stakeholders. Hence, the conceptualization of the two-way asymmetrical oversimplifies persuasion and negates the fact that someone trying to engage in persuasion can be changed by the information he or she collects.

The symmetrical model focuses on the balance between the organization and the stakeholder. It implies collaboration and cooperation between the organization and stakeholder. A dialogue, the exchange of messages, develops between them. "Symmetry induces a symbiotic relationship between organization and public; the two are equal partners, interdependently sharing information in order to arrive at mutual understanding" (Bowen 2005c: p. 837). Symmetry is not a static concept; rather, it is adjusted over time. There is negotiation between the organization and stakeholder. In symmetrical communication people do try to influence one another when engaging in conflict resolution and negotiation (Bowen 2005b).

But it is misleading to assume that a dialogue in symmetrical communication will not involve some form of persuasion. That would be like saying that information is purely distinct from persuasion. In reality, information is not really neutral. The selection of information, deciding what to present and how to present it (or frame it), can be used to persuade people – to change their attitudes or behaviors. The information we receive or do not receive shapes our view of the world and how we react to it. Therefore, it is difficult to imagine a situation where dialogue can be neutral and not favor some interests over others. The important point is that organizations and stakeholders may be partners in two-way communication *but rarely will they be equal in terms of power.*

We have discussed asymmetrical and symmetrical models to demonstrate that although the descriptions of the two models may sound good in theory, the distinction between them is not always clear. In two-way asymmetrical communication organizations can change as a result of listening to stakeholders; someone about to engage in persuasion is often changed by the information he or she collects from stakeholders. Further, in the dialogue in two-way symmetrical communication there can still be attempts to influence, and on the other hand, in some dialogues neither side changes at all. We feel the important point in both models is the willingness to listen.

As used here, "listening" doesn't mean simply hearing what others have to say. It also requires seriously considering or acting upon what stakeholders have to say. Mutual understanding and influence can occur through true dialogue. Merely giving lip-service to listening by "pretending to care" about the concerns of stakeholders is not truly listening. As we included in our definition of public relations as the management of mutually influential relationships, the relationship is *mutually influential* because both parties affect the cognitions and/or behaviors of the other. In other words, there is some degree of interdependence within the relationships.

Critiques of public relations, such as those presented in Chapter 1, often seem to assume a one-way view of communication (as well as influence) focusing on how PR professionals communicate with the public. Even the codes of ethics for the two professional organizations seem to emphasize one-way communication. In the one-way view of communication, a sender (the PR professional) is seen as sending a message to receivers (stakeholders, the public) who supply no feedback on their reactions. The communication functions as a monologue. This perspective is reflected in criticisms focusing on the potential power of PR to produce opinion change. In critiques, descriptions of public relations practitioners' use of VNRs (video news releases), press releases, and publicity campaigns typically reflect a one-way view of the communication and portray the receivers (the public) as rather passive and gullible.

In reality, two-way communication between PR professionals and stakeholders may be more the norm in both theory and practice. Organizations should be interested in the opinions and needs of stakeholders. Integrated marketing research has documented the shift in marketplace power from distributors to consumers. Consumers have greater power than before, since they are able to access a wider range on information about products and services, thanks to the Internet. Corporations, in turn, must respect this power and be sensitive to the needs of consumers (Schultz 2003). In order to supply products and services that are desired by stakeholders, organizations must pay attention to what they are saying they need and want from the organization. What can this organization offer to consumers? Does the organization supply what it says it will supply? Does it meet expectations?

We also must consider the broader context or environment in which the organization operates. Stakeholders may expand their concerns beyond the products and services offered by the organization; they may also be concerned with the way in which the organization operates. What sort of community citizen is it? How does it affect the local as well as the global environment? How does it treat its workforce? Does the organization support human rights everywhere it operates? Because an organization operates as a "public citizen" in the public arena, it is open for scrutiny. As a member of the community, the organization can be questioned on its citizenship behaviors. Does it contribute to the "public good"? If it operates globally, to what extent is it a good global citizen? The pressure for what is called *corporate social responsibility* (CSR) is growing.

At its core, CSR is the recognition that organizations have responsibilities to all of their stakeholders. It is no longer enough to meet financial responsibilities. Corporations must be cognizant of, and manage their effects on, social and environmental concerns (Rawlins 2005). CSR programs attempt to demonstrate what an organization has been doing to meet its social and environmental responsibilities. Chapter 5 will elaborate on the complex dynamics that surround CSR. Organizations are being called upon to justify their existence by demonstrating that they add value to society rather than exist for their own purposes. The PR professional can alert the organization to these CSR concerns and warn management when stakeholders perceive that the organization is acting unethically. Chapter 5 will provide additional insight into CRS demands by offering some specific case examples.

Tensions for PR Practitioners

From the preceding discussion it is clear that the realities of the business world place practitioners in a quandary. While the professional codes of ethics suggest that practitioners should favor the interests of society as a whole, the reality is that the practitioners work for the client. Who pays the practitioners' salaries? It may be unrealistic to expect PR professionals to disregard "who pays the bills" in favor of the public interest. Consider one of the early statements of public relations ethics, Ivy Lee's "Declaration of Principles." The "Declaration" was hailed as a sign of a seismic shift, from ignoring to embracing stakeholders. A key point was providing accurate information (Wilcox et al. 2000). However, when push came to shove, Ivy Lee sided with clients. During a Congressional investigation, Lee was asked what responsibility he had to make sure the information his clients asked him to disseminate was true. His response was "none" (Heath and Coombs 2006). Ultimately Lee viewed public relations as a delivery system for the client, not as a protector of the public.

Another source of tension is that exactly what constitutes "the public interest" may be debatable in a complex society. As we discussed earlier, there are multiple stakeholder groups that comprise that public. Certainly the public interest cannot be monolithic. What if these stakeholder groups pose different ethical standards? Which stakeholder groups should be emphasized? To which groups' concerns do we devote more attention? To what extent do the concerns of stakeholder groups conflict with one another such that pleasing one will agitate another? Who decides which groups are privileged over others? Shouldn't those groups that can more directly impact on the organization receive greater attention? The web of stakeholder relationships is complex and interdependent. Supporting that web requires skill. When making decisions with ethical implications, PR practitioners are likely to consider that complex web of relationships as well as issues pertaining to the power of stakeholder groups. The next section explores power and its potential to affect professional decision-making with respect to the organization, public opinion, and various stakeholder groups.

Power Relationships

Power is a central concept in the analysis of relationships, regardless of whether they are private and interpersonal (e.g., friendships, marital, familial relationships) or public (an organization and its stakeholders or publics). As noted by Leitch and Neilson (2001), "power is a key element in the analysis of social relationships in nearly all other disciplines... and in social theory generally" (p. 129). A consideration of power is important to discussions of the practice of public relations.

As we have discussed, relationships are characterized by perceptions of interdependence. There is some type of interconnection, some intertwining of behavior. If there is no interdependence, there is no relationship. When we perceive that another can influence our behavior (regardless of whether they choose to or not), then that other has power. People or groups have power when they can get another to do something they would not otherwise do. The other may act (or not act) because resources could be withheld or provided, actions could be thwarted or supported, or some other valued process or outcome could be affected. In this way power always is implicated in interdependent relationships. We can always ask: Who holds the most power in the relationship? Who could make the other behave in a particular way? Can stakeholders "make" an organization operate in a particular way or can an organization "make" stakeholders adapt to its policies and practices?

The robber barons of the early twentieth century did not change their ways and embrace public relations until stakeholders were able to leverage power and force change. We see that mirrored today in how Wal-Mart largely ignored critics until 2005. The growing influence of critical stakeholders on Wal-Mart's reputation and stock prices has resulted in a variety of changes to employment and environmental policies and practices at Wal-Mart as well as Wal-Mart engaging in a large-scale investment in public relations (McGinn 2005). Power (or more precisely, perceptions of power) is important because it explains how influence over another can be exercised.

In spite of the ubiquity of power, we are wary of it because it may be abused: it may make relationships unequal and inhibit or even dictate behavior. We often are uncomfortable talking about power because of our belief (in the United States, at least) that "all people are created equal," and inequities may be exposed that we would prefer to gloss over. However, we do in fact recognize the greater power that some people have, either in their own right or deriving from connections with powerful others, economic wealth, or attractive personal characteristics, etc.

Earlier we noted how the power to affect public opinion saddles practitioners with an ethical responsibility. When PR professionals consider their role as public communicators, they must consider the ethical implications of their words. They also must consider power: the power they have as organizational representatives to influence public opinion and on the other hand the power of the stakeholder groups that comprise the public. Corporations are assumed to have greater power than individuals or other groups because of their ability to gain access to the arenas of public discourse. For example, their economic resources enable them to purchase air time, produce VNRs and printed materials, host web sites, and orchestrate public events. These communication options are what enable them to get their concerns "out there" in the marketplace of ideas.When we consider stakeholder groups, we acknowledge that they also can exercise influence in the public domain. We see that some groups will be perceived to have more power than other groups, because of factors we mentioned, such as access to large numbers of like-minded people and economic resources. These powerful and influential groups are more likely to be on the "corporate radar" and in the public mind than the small, resource-poor groups. So while we think of corporations as being all-powerful we should consider how particular groups might accrue and exercise power and influence, enough to enter the marketplace of ideas, and influence public opinion as well. However, when compared to the corporations, their power is limited. Having power is critical in competing in the marketplace of ideas. In contrast, the public sphere is more of an ideal arena that is open to all citizens, whether powerful or not, and where ideas can be discussed and opinions formed; all voices are equal (L'Etang 1996). So here, public relations can be seen as a corrupting force (Bentele 2005). In the marketplace of ideas, however, the elite – the powerful – are privileged, and public relations has become an integral part of it.

The stakeholder groups can use their power to influence not just the public realm but also corporate activities. So while power will facilitate access to the public sphere, power also will allow access to other powerful groups. Stakeholder groups can challenge corporations, and those challenges, when publicized to generate awareness among the general population, become part of the marketplace of ideas. But that does not mean that all stakeholders are created equal. Some will be more salient to an organization than others. This means that the PR professional is likely to be motivated to attend to the issues raised by some groups more than by others.Organizations may listen to stakeholders not because they feel it is the "right thing to do" but because they believe stakeholders may disrupt their business operations if they don't. Corporations may listen for largely selfish reasons. For example, by listening, the organization may determine ways to satisfy enough of the stakeholder demands to prevent them from boycotting the organization. Corporations may agree to cooperate with stakeholders in finding alternative ways of operating. If the changes are acceptable to the organization and sufficient for appeasing stakeholders, it may be seen as a win-win situation. Also, an organization may listen simply in order to determine what is needed for them to be seen as more responsible. The current concern with corporate social responsibility demonstrates the sensitivity of businesses to criticism leveled at them for operating without regard for the public interest. When an organization helps the community, or groups such as schools and philanthropic associations, by donating money, products, or their employees' time, they also are helping themselves. Their CSR profile may be enhanced and they may deflect criticism of other aspects of their business operations.

Overall, power offers opportunities to access and influence the public domain. Power also influences the way in which corporations and stakeholder groups engage each other in public debate. Corporate resources generally carry much weight and can easily transfer into the kind of power large organizations need to achieve their purposes. So the advantage is certainly with the organization (L'Etang 1996).

The Power of PR Professionals in the Corporation

These discussions of power and ethics may create the impression that PR professionals are among the most powerful individuals within a corporation. In reality, that is usually far from the truth. They actually have relatively little power within the overall corporate structure. While we may think of them as providing the "voice of the organization," in reality it is more likely that they are simply doing as instructed by their superiors. Although textbooks will describe PR as a "management function," PR professionals often lack the significant decision-making power that undergirds management strategies. It is for their technical skills in crafting effective messages that the PR professionals are valued. Executives within the organization usually make the "big picture" decisions; they determine the strategy. Then the PR professionals are called upon to figure out the nuts and bolts of how to enact that strategy. From this angle the PR function doesn't sound very powerful. So while public relations practitioners may aspire to be a part of the dominant coalition, the group that makes decisions in most corporations, they are usually not included (Grunig 1992; Bronn 2001).

Typically, PR roles are actually limited to performing tasks related to message design and dissemination. PR executes the vision and strategy set out by executives. For example, while they do not plan the strategy, practitioners may determine how to say it and where to place these messages. Newsom et al. (2004) note that PR professionals are hired to be advocates for the organization. In reality, they typically aren't the ones determining exactly *what* should be advocated. But when management's strategic decisions prove to be disastrous, for example when a management plan is revealed to be problematic, illegal, or "ethically challenged," PR practitioners are called upon to "clean up the mess." It may in fact be be a mess that they anticipated. Perhaps they had warned management and their protests were not heeded because they were not part of the dominant coalition; they did not have the personal power to significantly alter the strategy.

As PR professionals are trying to execute the vision of upper management, they may be reminded of textbook descriptions of their role and ethical responsibilities. For example, Treadwell and Treadwell (2005) describe how public relations functions as the "conscience of the organization" and Newsom et al. (2004) suggest it operates as the "conscience of management." So in spite of the fact that PR professionals typically do not have the power to make significant strategic decisions for the organization, they may be seen as responsible for monitoring or for identifying the ethical considerations implicated in the decisions. In serving the needs of their clients, PR professionals are expected to accomplish the goals set forth by management while being vigilant in adhering to ethical guidelines. If they note possible ethical violations in the recommended strategy, they can identify those to management. However, they do not really have the authority to change it. They probably do not have have enough importance even to raise their concerns about an ethical problem. If they do voice those concerns about possible ethical violations, will it make a difference? Or will they be expected to find a way of justifying the breach of ethics? Everything considered, the power of PR professionals within the organization is really quite limited. They may not be able to truly let their conscience be their guide.

A Postmodern Perspective on PR

Viewing public relations from a postmodern perspective has been gaining in popularity, owing to postmodernism's overall influence across a wide array of disciplines. Postmodernism informs many aspects of our society, from literary movements to aesthetics to educational practices to organizational design (e.g., bureaucracies replaced by more flexible organizational forms). Postmodernism is quite complex and a complete explanation is well beyond the scope of this book. However, we can identify at least one important aspect of it that has been influential in thinking about PR functions and holds implications for its practice. Theorists who write about "postmodern PR" have been especially interested in how demographic and ideological shifts in society alter the PR playing field and how PR should respond to this diversity.

Descriptions of contemporary society often note it has grown more diverse along a number of factors, including culture, ethnicity, economics, and class. Along with this diversity has come a greater concern for democratic practices that recognize and value the different, often conflicting, "voices" that arise from this diversity. Wedded with the recognition of multiple voices comes the realization of the inevitable conflict prompted by these different experiences, beliefs, expectations, and values. Evaluations of what constitutes ethical practices may vary because of these differences in values and beliefs. Such disagreement among groups is to be expected. Groups compete to get their concerns and messages "out there" in the marketplace of ideas. They will be motivated to become activists in efforts to be heard – and hear others – in the political arena.

From a postmodern perspective, "the public good" should be viewed as highly contested terrain. Can there be *one* public good? How do we privilege the larger interests of society (the assumed "greater good" – compared to more micro organizational interests) when society is composed of diverse groups with different interests, needs, and claims?

Postmodern writers Holtzhausen and Voto (2002) note that PR is accused of acting unethically, and many incidents support them. Corrupt Enron executives used investor relations messages, a specialty field within public relations, as one mechanism in the scheme to generate personal wealth at the expense of investors. The Bush administration, through Ketchum Public Relations, paid "journalist" Armstrong Williams to promote the No Child Left Behind (NCLB) initiative on his show and to other news outlets. Armstrong never disclosed the arrangements when he was making endorsements for NCLB (Horton 2005). Postmodern public relations theorists suggest that we should conceive of PR as being able to perform a broader ethical role within society, working to insure that disparate voices both outside and inside the organization are heard by the organization. The ethic of care seems consistent with the postmodern perspective because it highlights the need to feel a sense of responsibility to others.

These writers contend that in the postmodern practice of public relations, the PR professional will act as an activist within the organization (Holtzhausen 2000; Holtzhausen and Voto 2002). They suggest that taking a more activist stance will make public relations more ethical (Holtzhausen 2000). What exactly would this look like? How would this work? It involves acting as an advocate for marginalized stakeholders as well as for the organization. This view of activism is consistent with the ethic of care. Holtzhausen (2000) suggests this requires PR professionals to function actively as change agents, to act as the "conscience" of the organization, and to give voice to those stakeholders who lack power in their relationships with the organization. The PR professionals will question management, which represents the dominant (capitalist) ideology, and represent the interests of external publics, and will not shy away from conflict but rather use it to create new ways of thinking and problem-solving (Holtzhausen and Voto 2002). They will recognize that management and its views are dominant and strive to move against that dominance by legitimizing the voices of those representing divergent perspectives that counter management views. The professional is more of a crusader or activist in the postmodern practice of PR. The clash of ideas is seen as beneficial to the organization as well as society.

As boundary-spanners, PR professionals are uniquely situated to be exposed to the different perspectives of diverse groups and therefore should be well suited to identifying conflicts. The postmodern view suggests PR practitioners should pay greater attention to stakeholders and not only enable those groups to become activists, but they should themselves perform activist roles on their behalf. It is important to monitor what various groups in society are thinking and doing with respect to the organization, its products and services, as well as to its competitors. PR practitioners can build good will across various segments of society by demonstrating a willingness to listen to different points of view and earnestly represent those to management. They can facilitate a dialogic process.

But is this asking too much of PR professionals? Can they perform the dual advocate role and fulfill the expectations of postmodern PR theorists? Can PR significantly and accurately represent these competing stakeholder groups to management? Can these groups really trust PR professionals, as representatives of the organization, to voice their concerns? Can PR challenge management (and the concomitant capitalist ideology) to change its practices to accommodate the interests of these groups?

The idea of recognizing conflict and using it to create new ways of thinking and problem-solving seems a desirable goal. But is it realistic? Can PR professionals perform this activist role by challenging the organization to hear the voices of those marginalized groups? Can they make the organization want to hear and respond to groups that may be perceived to pose little threat to business operations? Can PR professionals be granted the power required to promote these kinds of changes?

Again, the issue of power surfaces. We have already noted that PR professionals generally are not at a significant decision-making level in corporations; they are not part of the dominant coalition. Being able to make meaningful accomplishments in this vein requires power. Moreover, PR professionals are paid by the organization. Hearing the concerns of a variety of groups is time-consuming and costly. Is the organization willing to pay professionals to do this? What happens when stakeholder concerns work against what management sees as their primary interests? Won't the organization be motivated to listen closely only to the most powerful and influential of the stakeholders? Do PR professionals really have enough power to place the concerns of stakeholder groups before management? Might performing this activist role jeopardize their position when the organization is not prepared to listen or act on the stakeholders' concerns? Practitioners could quickly lose credibility with stakeholders. And the corporation may question their loyalty to the organization.

Perhaps the best we can hope for is that the powerful do not abuse their power. That is, corporations will allow PR professionals to play a primary role in allowing divergent voices to be heard. PR experts may be able to play a facilitator or instructional role in helping stakeholder groups understand how they can use PR techniques to their own advantage. Of course, the danger is that this may seem akin to "arming the enemy." After all, they may use PR resources against the organization. But if the goal is two-way symmetrical communication, the potential for meaningful dialogue is enhanced when the playing field is leveled.

Conclusion

Unfortunately there is no easy way to address the ethical concerns raised in this chapter. There is no magical code of conduct that will solve all ethical concerns experienced by public relations professionals. Anyone who offers the one-size-fits-all ethical solution is viewing the context of public relations too simplistically. From the postmodern perspective, ethics should stem from individual – or situational – decision-making by a moral individual rather than be guided by normative decision-making imposed by society. Normative decision-making reflects the belief system (or ideology) of those in power, benefits the privileged, and reinforces the status quo. We have proposed that the ethics of care best reflects our definition of public relations as managing mutually influential relationships within a web of stakeholder and organizational relationships. This perspective on ethics leads us to value relationships and see them as a way to facilitate mutual understanding.

The best advice is that public relations practitioners must listen and utilize two-way communication to be ethical. Two-way communication sets the stage for mutual influence. You cannot be influenced by a group if you never hear it. Learning what other actors expect you to do puts you in a position of being able to discuss those expectations. Chapter 5 explores the role of expectations in more depth. But this is the start of a difficult journey, not a simple conclusion. There are differences in perceptions of what constitutes ethical behavior. If this is the case, isn't it likely that some group will be displeased with whatever action is taken because, within their worldview, it is not ethical? This dilemma is reflected in adages such as "you can't please all of the people all of the time" and "damned if you do, damned if you don't." Compromises to please the most number of people may result in no one being completely satisfied with the ethics of an action.

The ethics of public relations ultimately lies in the *process* and the *people utilizing that process*. Even medicine has physicians who abuse patients for person gain. Ethics ultimately reside within the individual. People can choose to abuse any public communication method, and public relations is no exception. The ethical outcomes of public relations actions are governed in large part by the ethics of the practitioner, not the structure of the public relations practice or well-meaning codes.

3

Who Practices Public Relations?

Public relations is more than simple publicity. Moreover, public relations operates within the web of relationships that binds organizations and various stakeholders and stakeholders with one another. However, while public relations uses the term "relationships," typically the focus remains primarily on how organizations and corporations relate to their stakeholders. This "corporate-centric" view of public relations has dominated the way many scholars conceptualize the field. Their attention has focused on how corporations in particular use public relations to further their business success. How other types of organizations, particularly activist organizations, use public relations has been ignored.

The influence of the corporate-centric view is most evident when we consider how existing publications discuss the history of public relations and who practices public relations. This chapter begins with a discussion of corporate-centric histories on public relations. We then discuss how power should be seen as a central factor in organization–stakeholder relationships. Stakeholder theory will help clarify the complexities of the power dynamic. We then show how activists have exercised power and have used public relations since the early nineteenth century. The public relations activities of today's activists have been aided by the Internet. The corporate-centric view of public relations will thus be shown to neglect the full range of public relations practices.

W. Timothy Coombs and Sherry J. Holladay

Corporate-centric Histories of Public Relations

The extant histories of public relations take a decidedly corporate-centric view of the practice. Cutlip's tome *The Unseen Power* (1994) is an excellent example. Using the "great person format," Cutlip takes us through the evolution of modern public relations, starting at around 1900. We are led through the pantheon of public relations legends: Ivy Lee, one of the first true public relations practitioners who was famous for his working relationship with John D. Rockefeller; Edward Bernays, the self-proclaimed "father of public relations" who viewed the profession as a science; Arthur Page, who integrated public relations into management decision making at AT&T; John Hill, co-founder of one of the most successful public relations agencies; Carl Byoir, who refined the use of special events in public relations; Clem Whitaker and Leone Baxter, who pioneered the use of public relations in the political arena; and Earl Newsom, well known for his work with Ford Motor Company on labor issues. In addition to being public relations luminaries, all of these figures worked in support of large corporate interests. Even though Whitaker and Baxter were primarily political consultants, their work for the American Medical Association (AMA) to defeat President Truman's national health care plan did benefit "corporate America."

Cutlip's second book, *Public Relations History: From the 17th to the 20th Century* (1995), does provide a broader view. Oddly, this book is barely a third the size of *Unseen Power*. We discover the connection between politics and public relations, starting with the colonization of America through the American Revolution and westward expansion into the growing integration of public relations into national politics, including the Civil War. It could be argued that the use of public relations to support political efforts is largely corporate public relations. Both focus on the advancement of the status quo and the benefit of large organizations. The last two chapters in Cutlip's book address issues related to non-profits and the ability of public relations to promote social change. But there are a mere 27 pages out of 284 pages of text devoted to truly non-corporate views of public relations.

Most introductory textbooks follow the same corporate history of public relations. Table 3.1 provides a summary of how introductory public relations textbooks present the history of public relations. The

Table 3.1   Historical names in introductory textbooks on public relations

Name	Category
Stephen Langton	Government
Amos Kendall	Government
Harriet Beecher Stowe	Activism
P. T. Barnum	Business/Agency
George Parker	Business/Agency
Jay Gould	Business/Agency
Herbert Small	Business/Agency
Charles Smith	Business/Agency
Samuel Insull	Business/Agency
Theodore Vail	Business/Agency
E. H. Heinrichs	Business/Agency
George Westinghouse	Business/Agency
Thomas Edison	Business/Agency
Henry Frick	Business/Agency
Pendleton Dudley	Business/Agency
J. P. Morgan	Business/Agency
Cornelius Vanderbilt	Business/Agency
Andrew Carnegie	Business/Agency
John D. Rockefeller	Business/Agency
Upton Sinclair	Activism
Ida Tarbell	Activism
Lincoln Steffens	Activism
George V. S. Michaelis	Business/Agency
William Smith	Business/Agency
Ivy Ledbetter Lee	Business/Agency
James Ellsworth	Business/Agency
Rex Harlow	Education
Edward Bernays	Business/Agency
George Creel	Government
Arthur Page	Business/Agency
Doris Fleischman	Business/Agency
Carl Byoir	Business/Agency
John W. Hill	Business/Agency
Don Knowlton	Business/Agency
Earl Newsom	Business/Agency
Leone Baxter	Business/Agency and Government
Ralph Nader	Activism
Paul Garrett	Business/Agency

To appear on the list, the name had to be mentioned in at least two of the six introductory public relations textbooks that were reviewed. The periods of activity of these individuals are arranged in approximate chronological order, ranging, with the exception of Stephen Langton (d. 1228), from the mid-nineteenth to the early twenty-first century.

bulk of the histories is comprised of corporate examples and contain virtually the same mix of names, companies, and events. There is the occasional discussion of the Revolutionary War, westward expansion, and national politics.

This chapter is not an attempt to rewrite public relations history. Instead, we seek to illuminate the generally unseen contributions of activists to the development of public relations. This exploration of activism's connection to public relations begins with the notion of public relations as a reaction to attacks on business. This is followed by a discussion of power and marginalization in public relations. We then review the contributions of activism to public relations from the 1830s through to the modern-day applications of the Internet.

Antagonistic Views of Corporations and Activists

It is worth noting that these "corporate" histories of public relations focus on corporations using public relations to react to events in society. In the early 1900s, the robber barons were reacting to the muckrakers (early investigative journalists) and efforts to regulate business. The Rockefellers and the Gettys, powerful industry leaders, suddenly realized that public opinion did matter and so men such as Lee and Bernays were paid to shape public opinion toward corporate interests. Similarly, the 1960s saw a need to address social issues, such as the consumer and women's movements that were beginning to impinge on corporate interests. Part of the historical evolution attributed to the field of public relations is tied to activism. However, the activists were viewed as barriers to overcome or challenges to meet. Activists helped create the "need" for modern public relations.

If we shift the focus a bit, activism can be seen "as" modern public relations. In the 1960s activists utilized public relations to attract the attention of the corporate elite, developing and utilizing many of the modern tools of public relations. Granted, not all activist public relations tools can be used by corporations. Corporations rarely protest, though Mitsubishi tried it unsuccessfully during its failed battle over sexual harassment charges in the 1990s. Early public relations giants such as Ivy Lee explained to the robber barons the need to work with newspapers, the "new media" of the day. Activists were working with the media, a primitive form of media relations, and this was helping them win in the court of public opinion. Lee started a media relations effort to have Rockefeller, the owner of Standard Oil, featured in favorable news stories. Sometimes these were a result of Rockefeller's influence over editors, while others were more "honest" stories showing the caring Rockefeller giving dimes to children he met.

It is not until the mid-1990s that public relations researchers considered activists to be practicing public relations rather than simply posing an obstacle. This realization was hailed as an epiphany in the field. Strangely, the evidence had been there for nearly a hundred years! The public relations field simply lacked the motivation or frame of reference for taking the activist's perspective. This chapter explores reasons for the failure to treat activism as public relations and the need for making the transition from viewing the activist "as obstacle" to viewing the activist "as practitioner."

Power and Marginalization

As noted previously in Chapter 2, public relations research and the practice have largely ignored the issue of power. Foucault distinguishes between "power" and "power over," and his distinction is useful for illuminating further the power dynamic in public relations. Power means that the actions of A (an organization) affect the field of possible actions for B (a stakeholder) and vice versa. Basically, power can be taken as the ability to get someone to do something they otherwise would not do. An example would be Burger King issuing new guidelines for purchasing meat after the People for the Ethical Treatment for Animals (PETA) launched the Murder King Campaign. Would Burger King executives have executed the policy shift if PETA had not created a "bleeding" web site and negative media coverage of Burger King? We venture to guess not. PETA was exercising power; it changed how Burger King behaved.

Given that public relations involves mutually-influential relationships, power can characterize the connection between organization and stakeholder. In reality, organizations predominantly utilize "power over." For power over, A (an organization) modifies the field of B (a stakeholder).

The concept of power over recognizes that in the mutually-influential relationship, the organization generally has greater influence than stakeholders.

Excellence theory dominated public relations thinking in the 1980s and 1990s. It is premised on having a dialogue between the organization and stakeholders. This dialogue helps to identify and resolve problems in the organization–stakeholder relationship (Bowen 2005b). Public relations researchers operating from a critical perspective have questioned the utility of Excellence theory, including its failure to address the power imbalance between organizations and stakeholders (Rakow 1989; Coombs 1993; L'Etang 1996).

Excellence theory, however, chooses to downplay or dismiss the issue of power and power over. The argument is that activists have just as much, if not more power, than corporations. If this is the case, why be concerned (Grunig 2001)? Organizations and stakeholders will naturally engage in a dialogue. This Excellence theory conceptualization of the organization–stakeholder relationship still does not address the basic power-related issue of who controls the initiation of a dialogue. We see this as a primary weakness of Excellence theory. As Mumby (1988) notes, there is power in the ability to control the communication process. Excellence theory counters that a dialogue solves power problems. As Burrell (1996) warns, dialogue is a weapon of the powerful. This suggests that Excellence theory may offer a naive conceptualization of power in the organization–stakeholder relationship because it does not recognize that organizations have the upper hand when it comes to deciding whether, and under what conditions, to engage in dialogue.

As noted by Grunig and White (1992) and Grunig (2001), the asymmetrical model of public relations suggest that stakeholders' arguments can force organizations into a dialogue. The point is that public relations can be powerful enough to contest the power over exploited by a corporation. This is a valid argument and one we will expound on in this chapter. However, not all activists have the skill or resources necessary to generate power. Some argue that activists have power equal to corporations and that activists have greater access to public attention than corporations. In large part, the activist influence is attributed to the news media being enamored with activists and having an anti-corporate bias in news reporting. The news media may enjoy the *schadenfreude* (pleasure in another's misfortune) in revealing corporate misdeeds and be drawn to unusual and dramatic visual images such as protestors chained to fences or perching in trees. But societal structures, such as government policy-making and news sources, still favor organizations over activists. Activists must compete with a wide array of events and issues when trying to capture public attention. This competition occurs largely within the public area of news coverage (Ocasio 1997), with the Internet gaining in relevance as a public arena as well. Public attention is a scare resource, and in the quest for it, structural features of US society actually favor corporations over activists (Hoffman and Ocasio 2001).

To appreciate the power dynamic in the organization–stakeholder relationship more fully, we need to place the relationship in context. By "power dynamic" we mean the ability of stakeholders to muster the resources necessary to influence an organization's field of possible actions (or behaviors). Organizations never have just one stakeholder relationship at a time; they exist within a complex web or network of stakeholder relationships. This network includes stakeholders forming relationships with one another as well as with the organization. Figure 3.1

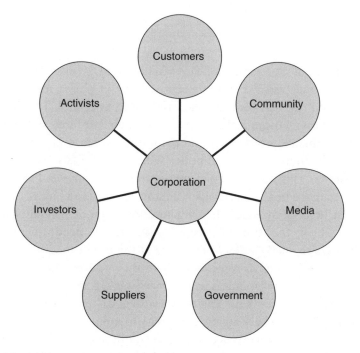

Figure 3.1   (a) Corporate-centric stakeholder network

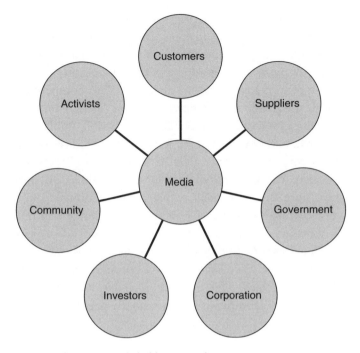

Figure 3.1 (b) Media-centric stakeholder network

offers a series of illustrations of the stakeholder networks. The first part of it shows the typical corporate-centric view of public relations. The second demonstrates how some view the media as central. The third and final part shows a more realistic view of the web that binds stakeholders. Excellence theory posits that the organization takes every stakeholder into consideration and communicates with each in a two-way symmetrical manner. This must also presuppose unlimited time and resources.

The management stakeholder literature takes a more realistic approach. It acknowledges that organizations cannot handle all stakeholders all of the time. Instead, organizations need to prioritize stakeholders regularly and address those at the top of the list. Managers focus the organizational resources where they will do the most good. This means some stakeholders will be marginalized and the organization will choose to ignore them. The organizations will pay greater attention to stakeholders who have a greater capacity to influence their operations.

Every stakeholder has power in the form of the threat to remove her- or himself from the relationship with the organization. Organizational

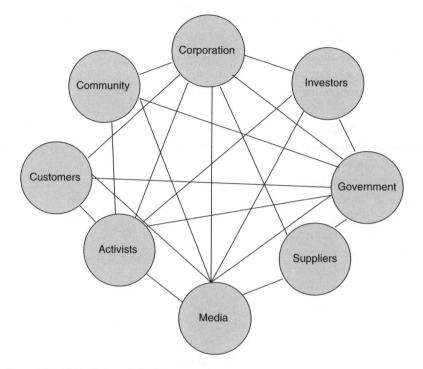

Figure 3.1   (c) Realistic stakeholder network

systems such as marketing and customer relations are designed to keep stakeholders in the relationship. By leaving a mutually-influential relationship, the stakeholder eliminates the organization's ability to exercise power over him or her. Why should an organization care if a stakeholder exits the relationship? The answer is that the organization is in fact harmed by the departure of a stakeholder, and the degree of harm reflects the power of the stakeholder. Harm can be both material and symbolic. "Material harm" refers to financial loss such as a drop in revenue or stock price, a loss of financial capital. "Symbolic harm" refers to loss of reputation or social capital. The two types of harm are related: reputations have financial effects on organizations while financial loss can damage reputations (Fombrun and Van Riel 2004).

Let us use customers to illustrate the point. One fewer customer does little material harm. However, a mass boycott of a product or service increases the potential material harm. However, boycotts rarely influence organizations through direct material harm. Boycotts succeed because organizations wish to avoid the reputational damage a boycott creates by its negative publicity. The negative publicity can cause the loss of social capital (symbolic harm) as well as intensify material harm. Numbers and public attention are valuable power resources for stakeholders. Organizations need to believe that a large number of stakeholders will become aware of and be influenced by a boycott or protest before changing their behaviors. So stakeholders need to be able to build power.

Although we have discussed organizations as having power, organizations do nevertheless depend to a greater or lesser extent on stakeholders. Clearly they depend on stakeholders for support. Customers must buy products or services, stockholders must invest money, and communities must provide favorable operating climates. In addition, organizations rely on stakeholders to refrain from interfering with their business or contesting their reputation. Challenges – or the potential for challenges – to either reputation or operations are problematic and may necessitate a response. Challenges can be traced back to conflicts of interests. If stakeholders perceive that an organization poses a threat to their interests they may decide to challenge the organization.

Stakeholder theory offers an explanation of how stakeholders come to be viewed as powerful and thereby important to management. In their review of the stakeholder literature, Mitchell et al. (1997) propose three dimensions for evaluating the salience of stakeholders: (1) *power* (the ability to get an actor to do something he or she would not do otherwise); (2) *legitimacy* (the perception of actions as appropriate, desirable, or proper within the context of some belief system); and (3) *urgency* (the extent to which the time frame is important, e.g. immediate action being called for because of the importance of the claim or the relationships to stakeholders) (Agle et al. 1999; Bryson 2004). Their proposal has been well received in the management literature (e.g., van Riel 2000). Stakeholder salience is a function of the ability to demonstrate these three attributes. High scores translate into a higher prioritization for the stakeholder. In other words, if management perceives activists to demonstrate these three attributes, management will feel pressure to deal with the stakeholders and their issues.

This is further complicated by the fact that the demands of different stakeholder groups are often contradictory or mutually exclusive. The

Table 3.2   Stakeholder categories (Mitchell et al. 1997)

Latent stakeholders: posses only one of three salience attributes.

    Dormant: power only
    Discretionary: legitimacy only
    Demanding: urgency only

Expectant stakeholders: posses two of the three salience attributes.

    Dominant: power and legitimacy
    Dependent: legitimacy and urgency
    Dangerous: power and urgency

Definitive stakeholders: posses all three salience attributes.

importance of various stakeholders can change depending on the situation (Newsom et al. 2004). The issues advocated by competing groups must be prioritized according to their threat level as determined by their ability to impact negatively on the organization and their probability of developing momentum. Mitchell et al. use their three factors to prioritize stakeholders and develop seven different categories of stakeholders, which are shown in Table 3.2. The higher the prioritization, the more likely organizational management is to address the relationship with the stakeholder. The highest priority goes to their "definitive" stakeholders because they possess power, legitimacy, and urgency.

Activists tend to populate the discretionary and dependent categories. There are, however, a few, elite non-government organizations (NGOs) that have power based on their years of activity, strong organizational structure, and communication skills. Greenpeace is one such elite NGO. We are working under the assumption that any activist group has a legitimate concern, in other words, that other stakeholders would agree the situation in question is a problem. Discretionary stakeholders have legitimacy but lack power and urgency. There is a legitimate problem but no rush to address it because little attention is focused on the issue. Organizational management has no pressing need to address their concerns. Discretionary stakeholders can be marginalized. Management often addresses discretionary stakeholders only out of a need for corporate social responsibility (Mitchell et al. 1997).

Dependent stakeholders possess legitimacy and urgency. These stakeholders depend on others because they lack power. The "others" could be additional stakeholders or members of an organization's own management team. One view in critical public relations is that the public relations person should be that "other" (Holtzhausen 2000). Still, organizational management can choose to marginalize dependent stakeholders. In other words, they can rank them a low priority. The "good news" in the Mitchell et al. system is that stakeholder salience is fluid. Power, legitimacy, and urgency can change over time, leading to a re-evaluation and re-prioritization of the stakeholder. We echo others in maintaining that public relations is a vital resource in controlling the process. This is important because activists will be perceived to have greater salience when the attributes of power, legitimacy, and urgency are strong (Coombs 2002).

The salience of a stakeholder has implications for trying to facilitate change. Changes in organizational behaviors can be voluntary or involuntary but both are driven by salience. For instance, an organization can willingly implement workplace anti-violence policies or be required to do so by government agencies. Pressure from stakeholders can also lead an organization, to change, a pressure stemming from the fear that stakeholders will leave the relationship. Companies are concerned to be socially responsible largely because so many stakeholders believe in the value of social responsibility. Thus, change can be driven by outside factors.

However, research in this area strongly suggests that someone or some group in an organization must support a change if it is, first of all, to happen, and secondly, to endure. As noted earlier, critical public relations theorists posit that public relations practitioners should be the internal advocate. But a PR internal would-be advocate is unlikely to be inspired by marginal stakeholders; their calls are easy to ignore and offer little incentive. To be successful, members of top management must publicly support the change as well.

Involuntary change is a result of policy decisions. Policy decisions take the form of laws or regulations. After decades of public service announcements about seat belt benefit, states simply made it a law that seat belts must be worn. Policy decisions can result from a mix of outside pressure and internal champions. Through media coverage, pressure can build on a government agency to take action. The public and media agenda do influence government policy (Gandy 1982; Kingdon 1984; Manheim 1987). Once a cause appears on the media and public agendas, it becomes well known and supported by a large number of people. There always has been power in numbers when it comes to policy-making. For example, the pressure to ban Alar, a chemical designed to improve the appearance of fruit, was an orchestrated effort designed to pressure the Environmental Protection Agency (EPA) through the media and public agendas. The news media portrayed Alar as evil and public opinion strongly favored its banning. The EPA eventually banned Alar even though there was little scientific data to support the action. (Chapter 4 explores the Alar case in greater detail.)

While media and public agendas can influence the policy agenda, there is no guarantee. A cause can gain media or public attention but never transfer to the policy agenda. One factor that can aid a cause is an inside champion. An *inside champion* is a powerful political actor who fights for the cause inside the policy-making machine. The inside champion realizes the issue has value for her or his political career. Research has shown that one key factor for a cause moving from the media and public agendas to the policy agenda was an inside champion (Arnold 1989). Another reason that marginal stakeholders find it difficult to affect media, public, or policy agendas Is that they lack the salience to build agendas that are attractive to inside champions.

The challenge for activist groups has always been how to move from the margin to claim the attention of organizational leadership. The movement from marginal to salient involves managing the mutually influential relationships, and encouraging management to recognize that the stakeholder is gaining influence. Both traditional and non-traditional public relations tactics can be used to attract the public attention necessary to do this. The more people there are who know about the concern, the greater the likelihood of yet more people adding their support (Crable and Vibbert 1985). And the more people, especially high profile people, who support a cause the greater the perceived power of the activist group. This is why modern activists allocate time to training in the media and in Internet use, the better to reach and mobilize people (Ryan 1991). We will give examples of activists using public relations in the past and later using the new communication technology as it evolves. This journey will demonstrate that there is a history and tradition in activism that began some time before the modern corporation.

W. Timothy Coombs and Sherry J. Holladay

First Reform Era: Abolitionism and Temperance

In the 1830s and 1840s, the United States witnessed its first wave of organized efforts to bring about social reform. These reformers fought to correct social ills such as slavery (the abolitionists) and the negative social consequences of excessive drinking (the temperance activists).

The abolition movement in the US emerged in the 1830s as an extension of the Second Great Awakening, a religious revivalist movement of the time. Slavery was associated with sin and emancipation was the way of repentance. In 1831, brothers Arthur and Lewis Tappan formed the Anti-Slavery Society in New York. Two years later the society became nation-wide. The Anti-Slavery Society sought to reach a wide audience with its message and to develop support for emancipation. The Society used public meetings, petitions, printed leaflets, posters, journals, sermons, and public lectures to reach their target audiences. One of the prominent orators was Sojourner Truth. She was a New York slave who had been freed when the state abolished slavery in 1827. By 1840, the Society had over 2,000 local chapters, 250,000 members, and had published over twenty journals (Anti-Slavery Society, 2005). Even literature was used as a communication channel. Harriet Beecher Stowe's *Uncle Tom's Cabin* was considered an effective persuasive device. The book brought the abolitionist message into the homes of white America and converted many to the cause ("I will be heard," 2005).

That same year, the Tappans lead created a splinter group known as the American and Foreign Anti-Slavery Society. They, and other men in the Anti-Slavery Society, did not approve of the growing role of women in the abolitionist movement. Women were now speaking in public and serving on the Society's executive board. Among them were the abolitionists Amelia Bloomer and Susan B. Anthony, They also strove for women's suffrage. There was an overlapping of social issues and activists in the 1800s. Today, it is hard to imagine that the abolitionists were very unpopular and faced stiff opposition when they first started speaking on the issue. These brave individuals still carried their persuasive message to others. Eventually a strong political element of abolitionists emerged through lobbying and political parties. Abolitionists helped to make emancipation one of President Lincoln's goals in the Civil War (Anti-Slavery Society, 2005).

Temperance activists were at first contemporaneous with abolitionists but the movement extended beyond the 1800s to the 1900s. Temperance was much more than a matter of banning the sale of alcohol. Excessive drinking was seen to be linked to many social problems, including domestic abuse, severe health problems, and crime. Because women often bore the brunt of the alcohol-related problems they were among the leaders of temperance efforts. Temperance and women's rights were intertwined, hence leaders such as Susan B. Anthony were significant figures in both causes. Temperance was not an issue confined to the United States. Ireland, Scotland, England, Norway, and Sweden all experienced extensive temperance efforts. In the US, temperance activities began as early as 1808 and extended into the early 1900s with the passage of the 18th Amendment (Prohibition) in 1919. Among the items on the agenda were government control over alcohol and education on alcoholism in schools. Temperance activists were issue managers. They used communications strategically in order to shape public policy decisions. A closer look at their activities will illustrate how these activists were practicing public relations.

The practice of public relations cannot be separated from the channels of communication. During the heyday of the temperance movement, the primary channels were public speeches and events, sermons, and minor publications. As with issues management today, activists needed to create public awareness of the problem and support for their solutions to the problem. Communication is the tool for creating awareness and building support. Modern public relations practitioners often create what historian Daniel Boorstin calls "pseudo-events." A pseudo-event is designed in part to attract attention. Today it is the media whose attention is attracted. In the 1800s the focus was on public attention: people coming out to witness an event. Temperance activists would hold large outdoor meetings and parades, picket to stop delivery of alcohol, and engage in civil disobedience to draw attention (Schienderman 2005). The Women's Christian Temperance Union and Carry A. Nation (2005) illustrate the public relations efforts of the temperance activists.

The Women's Christian Temperance Union (WCTU) was founded in 1873. Its crusade was born with a pseudo-event in Hillsboro, Ohio. On Christmas Eve of 1873, Mrs Eliza Thompson, a respected woman in the community, led seventy women from praying on their knees in a local Presbyterian church to the nearby saloons. Singing "Give to the winds thy fears," the women marched two-abreast into drinking establishments and prayed for the wayward souls. Mrs Thompson and her followers repeated this act throughout the town. If they could not get into an establishment, they prayed in front of it in the snow. Eventually all of the establishments that sold liquor agreed to stop selling alcohol. This became the model for other chapters of the WCTU to follow.

Mrs Thompson's efforts were very effective at generating publicity and spreading the word. Early publications in Cincinnati, Chicago, and New York covered the event. *Harper's Weekly,* an influential publication at the time, ran stories and cartoons about the events. The Ohio crusade became a staple part of temperance speeches and was even noted in sermons. The available communication channels were being brought to bear on the problem (Crusades, 2005).

In 1881, Kansas became the first state to outlaw the sale and production of alcohol. The laws in Kansas were unevenly enforced to say the least. Men were still able to drink and the social problems related to alcohol abuse continued in the state. As early as 1855, women in Kansas were smashing bars. But Carry A. Nation knew the public relations value of this action. Carry Nation's first husband, Charles Gloyd, was an alcoholic. His drinking ruined their marriage and eventually claimed his life. She later married David Nation. After they moved to Medicine Lodge, Kansas, she began her crusade against alcohol. At first she tried legal means. After all, it was illegal to sell alcohol in Kansas. After limited success, Carry Nation heard a voice in a dream that inspired her to smash saloons. She began by throwing rocks and then switched to her well-known hatchet.

Carry A. Nation was not a crazed woman listening to voices in her head. Her actions were calculated and designed to build attention and support for the temperance cause. Carry trademarked her name, sold little pewter hatchet pins to cover her fines, traveled widely to lecture on the evils of alcohol, published a newsletter titled "The Smasher's Mail," and continued to smash salons with a hatchet. She was known as "the Lady with the Hatchet." She used her notoriety to spread her cause. Carry Nation's actions were a calculated attempt to make people aware of the social problems of alcohol and the need to ban its sale. Today, Carry Nation would be viewed as engaging in guerrilla public relations (Carry A. Nation, 2005).

Many well-crafted issue management efforts fail. Political scientists note that having powerful allies helps to move an issue forward and to create public policy (Arnold 1989). An important function of these messages that communicate about an issue is coalition building. The temperance activists found allies in the business community. Business leaders wanted to support their cause because hung-over workers were costing them money. Heavy drinking resulted in workers being absent and having accidents. Business leaders viewed temperance as a means of improving productivity. Women saw it as a way to combat social ills and to save money. It was not uncommon for men to drink away over one half of their wages in the 1800s.

Public relations aspect

In the 1800s, the term "public relations" did not exist, but that does not mean the activity of public relations did not exist. Stakeholders existed, there was mutual influence, and actors did try to manage the mutually influential relationships. Part of public relations involves using communication to shape public opinion in order to influence public policies. Temperance and abolitionist activists were using public relations to create pressure for social change. Activists of this era employed the print media, public speeches (including sermons), and pseudo-events to draw attention to and build support for their cause. The activists in the First Reform Era were strategically using communication in a sustained effort to combat the social evils of alcohol by influencing public opinion. We need to consider these early activists as practicing public relations.

Second Reform Era: The Muckrakers

Accounts vary, but the Progressive Era in the US ran from about the 1890s until the 1920s. Prohibition and women's suffrage, two First Reform Era issues, reached maturation during this time. The US was undergoing a significant social transformation. Industrialization, urbanization, and immigration were altering the basic social fabric of society. The transformation brought crime, poverty, disease, and corruption as well as changing how people worked and lived. The problems of the transformation led many to demand additional changes.

Socialism emerged as one of the voices for change. The socialists wanted to eliminate capitalism and the "disease" it spread, and they found eager converts among the poor and working class. Their radical ideas led to many heated and violent conflicts between capitalists and socialists, mostly in the form of labor strife. Progressives sought to reform the ills of society through the existing society. They were middle- and upper-class citizens, who put their faith in the power of educated individuals who are dedicated to a cause. A variety of non-profit organizations were created to address societal ills. A new breed of investigative journalists arose from the clamor of the Progressive Era: the muckrakers.

From 1900 to 1915, the muckrakers were a catalyst for changing American society. Their writings produced such varied reforms as child labor laws, the dissolving of Standard Oil, the conservation of natural resources, and workmen's compensation laws. Today these varied writers are collectively known as muckrakers. "Muckraker" is a derogatory term used by their one-time ally President Theodore Roosevelt. Roosevelt was driven to reform and election by the concerns raised by muckrakers. However, when muckrakers revealed inappropriate actions by Roosevelt supporters in the Senate, the President changed his tune. In a 1906 speech, Roosevelt said the investigative reporters were like the muckrakers in Bunyan's *The Pilgrim's Progress*. They only stared down at their muck and could not see the celestial crown overhead. After Roosevelt's label was applied, the muckrakers experienced a decline in readership and influence, from a peak in 1906 of over 3 million readers (Muckraking, 2005).

Muckrakers are considered the impetus for modern public relations. The corporate leaders of the day, known as robber barons, hired public relations people such as Ivy Lee to combat the negative publicity and public opinion generated by the muckrakers. Muckrakers used the printed word as their means of informing and persuading people about social issues. They used a mix of books, newspapers, and magazines. Upton Sinclair and Ida Tarbell serve to illustrate how muckrakers reached and influenced others with their words.

Upton Sinclair was a socialist who wanted to improve US society. In 1904, he was commissioned by the socialist publication *Appeal to Reason* to write a book about the poor working and living conditions of immigrants who serviced the Chicago meat packing industry. Sinclair lived among the workers for seven weeks to understand their plight. He was appalled by how these people were treated. The result was *The Jungle*. His writings were serialized in *Appeal to Reason* in 1905. However, Sinclair wanted to take the plight of these workers to a broader audience.

The problem was that no one wanted to publish the book. Six different publishers turned him away. They feared the message of social change Sinclair advocated. Sinclair pressed on and announced in *Appeal to Reason* that he would publish the book himself. When Doubleday learned that he had 972 orders, the company agreed to publish *The Jungle*. It sold over 150,000 copies in the first year. It was eventually published in 17 languages and was a best-seller around the world.

The Jungle inspired President Theodore Roosevelt to investigate the meat packing industry. He and other Americans were horrified by the unsanitary conditions of the facility and the abuse of its workforce. The Pure Food and Drug Act (1906) and the Meat Inspection Act (1906) were attributed to Sinclair's efforts. Sinclair himself was less than excited. His goal was to help the workers and that did not transpire. He lamented aiming for people's hearts but instead hitting their stomachs. Even the two Acts were more style than substance. The names reassured the angry American public that their meat was safe. Little actually changed in the industry but the Acts created quiescence among consumers (Upton Sinclair, 2005).

Ida Tarbell did not have the crusading passion of Upton Sinclair but was a leading muckraker nonetheless. Tarbell's *The History of Standard Oil* was an exposé of John D. Rockefeller's unethical and often illegal business practices. First published as a nineteen-part series in *McClure's* magazine, a leading muckraking publication, it later became a book that has been recognized in the top five of the most important works by twentieth-century journalists (People & Events, 2000). Prior to muckraking, Tarbell had been a well-known biographer writing books about Napoleon and Abraham Lincoln. *The History of Standard Oil* was a carefully documented work based on court records and interviews with both victims of, and workers for, Standard Oil. She even gave an advance copy to Standard Oil management for comment. Rockefeller referred to her as "Tarbarrel." Tarbell was victorious in the end, since Standard Oil fell victim to trust busting (the breaking up by government of a monopoly). Rockefeller's oil empire was dismantled.

Tarbell had an agenda like other muckrakers. Her father had been in the oil industry in western Pennsylvania and was ruined by one of Rockefeller's early predatory practices, the South Improvement scheme. Tarbell had a distaste for Rockefeller, and so pitched the idea of an exposé of the oil industry to *McClure's*. She described Rockefeller as money-mad, a hypocrite, and a living mummy. Tarbell's careful investigative journalism reflected a particular point of view (People & Events, 2000).

Public relations aspect

The muckrakers used the growing print media to reach people. Through their exposés, muckrakers raised awareness of various causes and rallied people to them. Stakeholders moved from quiescence to agitation against large corporations. The power of the mass media as a tool for influencing stakeholders emerged. Sinclair and Tarbell are but two examples of how publicizing an issue can result in government reform and societal changes. Muckrakers used public communication to pursue objectives and influence relationships. It was by combating them on behalf of corporations that Ivy Lee established his reputation; his efforts were reactions to the muckrakers. The muckrakers were the first to understand the utility of the mass media.. These "original" public relations practitioners of the first half of the twentieth century encouraged corporations to become involved in influencing stakeholders. A public relations device (publicity) pioneered by activists was assimilated into the corporate world. Early publicists had simply brought their own take to the subject.

Saul Alinsky: Activism in the 1960s

The stockyards of Chicago gave birth to another great reformer: Saul Alinsky. While researching juvenile delinquency in the area, Alinsky decided he had to shift from watching to acting. He developed a model of community-based organizing; it would be to teach a community how to unite and to fight for its rights. He became a central figure in numerous community-action efforts in the 1960s, including those in Buffalo, New York, Kansas City, Missouri, and among the migrant workers in California. Clearly Alinsky was not the only activist or radical at work in the 1960s. However, he articulated a vision of activism that correlates with public relations more strongly than theirs did. Alinsky would use non-traditional public relations to attract publicity and put pressure on the power elites in communities. His publicity efforts were designed to prove that a community was united and a force to be addressed. His work in Rochester serves as an excellent example.

For many people, Rochester, New York means one thing: Eastman Kodak. The Kodak company built and controlled Rochester for decades. It was suspected of discrimination in hiring workers, and in 1964 became the focal point for a series of race riots that tore the town apart. The Rochester Area Council of Churches, a collection of white and black clergy, asked Saul Alinsky for help in extracting concessions for the workers from Kodak. The invitation was enough to ignite an initial firestorm of publicity. Newspapers and radio stations condemned the inviting of a hatemonger who could only make the situation worse. When the conservative news media turned against Alinsky, the black community decided they definitely needed Alinsky.

When he arrived at the airport, Alinsky was asked why he would work against Kodak, a company that had given so much to the black community. Alinsky replied, "Maybe I'm uninformed, but as far as I know the only thing Kodak has done on the race issue in America is to introduce color film." Alinsky formed a community group known as FIGHT (Freedom, Integration, God, Honor, Today). He planned the first ever "fart-in." Rochester's elite, among whom were Kodak managers, loved their symphony orchestra. The plan was to buy 100 tickets for protesters for a concert when the music would be soft, feed them baked beans before it began, and have them pass gas, loudly, throughout the performance. Talk of the "event" put some pressure on Kodak.

Traditional tactics placed greater pressure on Kodak. Starting with the General Assembly of the Unitarian-Universalist Association, Alinksy began collecting proxy votes for Kodak's upcoming annual meeting. Reports of FIGHT receiving over 5,000 shares raised concern. Soon many other religious organizations and supportive individuals were signing over proxies to FIGHT. Kodak designated FIGHT as the official representative of the Rochester black community and began to change its hiring practices.

Alinsky's second book, *Rules for Radicals*, outlines his process for effective community organizing. His advice is to keep in mind that community organizing is issues management. The organized community will agitate for change. His fifth chapter is titled "Communication" and opens as follows: "One can lack any of the qualities of an organizer — with one exception — and still be effective and successful. That exception is the art of communication" (Alinsky 1971: 81). Many of the comments in his chapter fit perfectly with writings on public relations. Communication, for instance, is viewed as a two-way process.

The central role of communication for Alinsky is to create understanding, a point shared with public relations. To create understanding, a communicator needs to know the stakeholders. Alinsky believed you could know the stakeholders through experiences. People only understand things through their own experiences. Hence, an organizer must discover and work within the experiences of the people he or she is targeting. "Since people understand only in terms of their own experience, an organizer must have at least a cursory familiarity with their experience" (1971: 84). Through this knowledge the organizer understands the stakeholders' values and goals. These values and goals then become the focal point of the messages. Alinsky is describing the process of using research to better understand and to more effectively communicate with stakeholders, ideas very germane to public relations.

Public relations aspect

Saul Alinsky understood the notion of power. Corporations and governments have it while community groups need to acquire it if they are to create change and promote dialogue. "It is only when the other party is concerned or feels threatened that he will listen" (1971: 89). Alinksy also knew that publicity, along with organizing, would help to build power. *Rules for Radicals* is in many respects a public relations primer for activists with its focus on communication as a mechanism for influence. In addition, Alinksy often used public communication as a means to re-shape relationships and corporate actions. As they had seen with the muckrakers, corporations in the 1960s needed to bolster public relations efforts in response to the demands of activists such as Alinsky.

Internet Activism

In the late 1990s, the Internet emerged as an important tool for activists. For example, the Nike exposé of sweatshops in Asia began in cyberspace. A consumer web site was instrumental in forcing Ford to recall hundreds of thousands of cars and trucks whose ignition switches could cause a fire in the vehicle. Human rights activists rallied online support that forced PepsiCo out of Myanmar (Burma) (Coombs 1998; Heath 1998). The Internet was the next evolution in communication technology. It has established itself as one of the channels used to spread the word about an issue and to rally support for a cause.

The American Family Association (AFA) offers an excellent example of how activists utilize the Internet. The AFA is a very conservative organization that seeks to promote and protect its view of traditional family values. It was founded in 1977 by Reverend Don Wildmon and claims over 2 million members. The AFA is attempting to clean up the entertainment industry by pressuring advertisers. It has been able to force a number of companies to stop advertising on certain television shows with threats of boycotts and the resultant negative publicity. The list of targets includes Burger King, Clorox, and S. C. Johnson. The AFA has expanded its operations beyond changing television content to encompass the policies of corporations, to bring them in line with its own view of traditional family values. This translates into the AFA attacking corporations it perceives to support a homosexual agenda. Companies such as Disney and Kraft have felt the wrath of the AFA for providing medical benefits for same-sex partners (General Information, 2005). This is where our story begins.

In June of 2005, the AFA called upon people to boycott Ford Motor Company and its related lines of vehicles. The AFA was seeking to reform Ford's pro-homosexual agenda. Ford was a significant sinner in the eyes of the AFA, for not only did it provide same-sex benefits but it donated money to homosexual organizations, helped to sponsor homosexual events, and had even created advertisements targeted toward homosexual car buyers. The AFA boycottford.com web site noted: "If one looks for the company which has done the most to affirm and promote the homosexual lifestyle, he would be hard-pressed to find a company which has done more than Ford Motor Company. While this is hardly known to the general population, it is well known by numerous homosexual organizations." The AFA planned to make Americans aware and angry through a campaign conducted largely on the Internet.

The AFA's boycottford.com site was a compilation of documents exposing and indicting Ford's pro-homosexual agenda. The evidence included statements of tolerance from Ford's internal documents, lists of pro-homosexual events sponsored by Ford, and links to web sites that discuss and have examples of Ford's gay-themed advertisements. The extensive use of links plays to the strength of the Internet: connectivity. People can easily access and navigate through the "evidence." Ford did not deny any of the claims. The company is proud that it preaches tolerance internally and provides same-sex benefits for employees; its sponsorships and advertising is part of an effort to tap into the lucrative gay market. Word of the boycottford.com web site spread rapidly through the Internet. Within three days, over 700 web sites had links to the AFA site. After one week, the AFA suspended its boycott after meeting with Ford dealers. The Ford dealers were given the deadline of December 1, 2005 for having Ford address the AFA concerns. If the dealers failed, the boycott would resume.

Critical web sites, also known as *attack sites*, are but one Internet channel that activists can develop. Other prominent channels include listservs, discussion groups, and weblogs. A listserv is an e-mail list that allows activists to send an e-mail to everyone on the list. The AFA calls its listserv AFA Action Alerts. The AFA can tell people when and how to act. The e-mail and its web site contain links to politicians to make it easier for people to send messages to targeted politicians. People can click and type rather than search for an address. The easier a course of action is, the more likely it is that someone will follow it. The AFA message was also posted to discussion groups about cars, trucks, and politics. People wrote weblogs (blogs) about the AFA boycott as well. Unfortunately for the AFA, the blogs and discussion postings were mostly supportive of Ford. Still, the AFA action illustrates how an array of Internet channels can be mustered in a public relations campaign that targets a corporation.

Granted, the AFA is a large activist organization. However, much smaller groups have also shaped corporate policies through the Internet. A web site developed by a couple in Georgia facilitated the Ford recall in the 1990s. A small group of dedicated anti-Myanmar activists were instrumental in PepsiCo leaving Myanmar (Coombs 1998). The Internet has the potential to draw attention and supporters to an issue. There are even sites dedicated to training activists how to use the Internet for public relations. Two examples of Internet training for activists can be found at http://netaction.org/training/ and http://www.actionpa.org/activism/. News media coverage of their Internet activities only intensifies the effect, for it drives more people to the web sites or postings. Organizations often change their behaviors rather than face the negative information that flows on the Internet and finds its way into the mainstream news media. But using the Internet communication channels is not a guarantee of success. There is a massive amount of information on the Internet so it is easy for messages to go unread. Nevertheless, modern activists are far from deterred from exploiting its public relations potential.

Public relations aspect

Internet activism exercises influence through the sustained efforts to shape public thinking. Traditional and non-traditional public relations devices are used. Traditional devices adapted for the Internet include news releases and public statements. The online traditional public relations tools include web pages, discussion groups, listservs, and blogs. Non-traditional devices include boycott and attack web sites. Corporations do not call for boycotts or develop attack web sites. As with the use of publicity in the early twentieth century, activist-based public relations online has been ahead of corporate public relations. Activists were orchestrating public relations efforts through discussion groups and blogs well before corporations realized their relevance and incorporated them into the mix of public relations and marketing communication. Again, corporate public relations learned the value of public relations devices from activists. Consider how giants such as Intel, Shell, and Ford re-thought public relations after experiencing the power of online public relations first hand.

Labor Unions and Public Relations

The public relations-related history of labor unions in the US largely parallels that of activists. The struggle between labor and management infuses the history of public relations (Cutlip et al. 1994). Unions were first formed in the early nineteenth century. To recruit and inform their members they needed means of communication, so many of them printed their own magazines and newsletters. These early days were marked by bloody confrontations between labor and management. The Great Railroad Strike of 1887 resulted in sixteen strikers being killed. The Homestead Strike of 1892 (at a steel plant near Pittsburg) was a four-month battle between labor on one side and the Pinkerton guards and local law enforcement on the other. Unions were fighting to improve the horrific working conditions. Safety and sanitation did not even rise to the level of an afterthought at this time (Manheim 2001).

The 1900s witnessed a shift from warfare to negotiation, although violence still did occur. An example is the Ludlow Massacre. Early in 1914, union members were on strike against the Colorado Fuel and Iron Company. They and their families were living in a tent city outside of Ludlow, Colorado, forced to stay outside the town because the company owned the towns. Tension was high since the strike had lasted much longer than expected. In April, National Guardsmen fired on the tents, killing two women and eleven children (Raucher 1968). Working conditions remained poor for employees. Another example is the Waist factory fire of 1911. A total of 145 men and women, mostly women, died when the Triangle Waist Companies shirtwaist-making facility in New York City caught fire. Some were smothered, some suffocated, and some jumped to their deaths (Echoes from the triangle fire, 1911). The fire attracted media attention and reinforced the idea that working conditions in factories often endangered the health and safety of employees.

The passage of the Railroad Labor Act guaranteed labor the right to organize and to bargain. More negotiation began to occur as this and other legislation protected the rights of unions. Labor unions experienced their golden age between 1933 and 1955, reaching the height of their political and economic influence (Manheim 2001).

Since the late 1950s, labor unions have waned in numbers and power in the US. The decline is epitomized by the Professional Air Traffic Controllers Organization (PATCO) strike in 1981. President Reagan fired the striking members of PATCO, effectively "killing" the union. The media supported the President by vilifying PATCO. Unions began to shift tactics from strikes to corporate campaigns. A corporate campaign is a research-based, long-term, and coordinated action that attacks a corporation's reputation in order to change its behavior. Corporate campaigns are a mix of media advocacy (publicity), boycotts, and attempts to influence the votes of shareholders (Manheim 1987). The work of many activist groups today can be described as corporate campaigns.

Public relations aspect

From their inception in the US, labor unions realized the value of public relations. The early confrontations with management were designed to, and did, elicit public sympathy for the workers. Today, unions join with many activists in corporate campaigns. Corporate campaigns are public relations. Various channels are used to reach stakeholders and change their perceptions of a corporation, that is, to erode its reputation. Moreover, labor unions have long used internal public relations to garner and to retain members. While we present them separately, unions and activists share many elements. Their histories are interwoven into the tapestry that is the history of public relations, and a result, we group unions with social activists in our expanded view of who practices public relations.

Conclusion

Social activists did not magically become public relations practitioners in the 1990s. This shift in thinking is an extension of the corporate-centric view of public relations. In reality, social activists were practicing public relations before large corporations existed. The public relations work of social activists spurred the growth of corporate public relations. Social activists, like any stakeholder, can utilize communication in their efforts to influence organizations and other stakeholders, that is, to manage mutually influential relationships. Any actor in the complex web of relations that includes organizations can practice public relations. We should examine the full realm of what constitutes public relations, not just the more traditional communication tactics organizations use to manage their mutually influential relationships. Moving beyond corporate-centric views and broadening the scope of who practices public relations enriches both the history and practice of public relations.

4

Public Relations Influences Society

Thus far we have considered public relations as it involves organizations and their stakeholders. As part of that discussion, we have noted that public relations has an effect on society. But what about situations where public relations is being used specifically to *shape* society? Public relations plays a very active role in strategic efforts to change and to prevent change to our society.

Marketplace of Ideas

Earlier we talked about the metaphor of the marketplace of ideas. In the US, the marketplace embodies the notion of freedom of expression. People are exposed to, and can express, a wide range of ideas. These ideas compete and the ideas that best suit the people win. Most public relations research is based on this metaphor directly or indirectly. Heath (2005) ties the rhetorical tradition in public relations directly to the marketplace of ideas. People use public relations to articulate their ideas. Ultimately the most attractive idea wins. Even Excellence theory is indebted to the metaphor. As we discussed in Chapter 2, in Excellence theory two-way symmetrical communication, the give and take of dialogue, endorses the exchange of ideas in the marketplace. However, the theory posits that conflict can be avoided as the various parties seek common ground and resolve their differences (Grunig 2001). As critics of Excellence theory have noted, parties may not always have a point of agreement or may find it in their best interests to *not* agree (Murphy and Dee 1992).

The marketplace of ideas is often a contentious venue, and social activism is one of the areas with the potential for conflict. Although many in public relations believe that corporations can learn a great deal from social activists, others still label them as the enemy. It has been recommended that the weapon of transparency be turned against them, to reveal how activists spend their money. a tactic that definitely treats activists as opponents (Irvine 2004). Thus opposing forces muster their communication resources in order to wield influence. Each tries to influence the other actors so that the social web reflects their desired view of reality. In question can be important policy decisions and social values that can affect stakeholders. For example, will the air we breathe be made cleaner, and thus cause industry extra expense? Will corporations be expected to meet certain minimum standards in behavior to be considered socially responsible?

Battles in the marketplace of ideas hinge on two dynamics, quiescence and arousal. Change depends on both. Quiescence is a word used in cell biology to denote the state of a cell when it no longer divides. In public relations, quiescence is the absence of formal opposition: people are not taking action against something. An unopposed idea is more likely than an opposed one to win in the marketplace, but support must be aroused, action stimulated, for the idea to be realized. If on the other hand the status quo is required, quiescence, a state of inactivity or apathy, might be encouraged (e.g., people are made to feel their actions will make no difference). This is a strategy used by totalitarian regimes to forestall any opposition. Again, if stakeholders are in fact happy with the way things are, there is no need or desire for change. Depending on whether change or the status quo is desired, public relations resources can be deployed to create either arousal or quiescence. Public relations should not, however, be used to silence voices. Box 4.1 examines steps some have taken to wrongly suppress voices, actions that should be condemned by those in public relations. As discussed in Box 4.1, SLAPPs (Strategic Lawsuit Against Public Participation) can silence opposition.

It is through the marketplace of ideas that society is changed. If people accept new ideas there is change. If people support the status quo, there is no change. History proves that society does change. Women now vote, slavery was abolished, the protection of the environment is a societal value, and corporations are held to a higher standard of financial reporting. Public policy and social marketing are the two major avenues

---

Box 4.1   SLAPPs as a threat to the marketplace of ideas

The marketplace of ideas is premised on the free flow of communication. The free flow of communication is the lifeblood of public relations because it is how influence is enacted. Any threat to the free exchange of ideas should be condemned by public relations practitioners as unethical. One information suppression strategy some times employed by corporations is the Strategic Lawsuit Against Public Participation or SLAPP. SLAPPs sue people for speaking on a public issue. The result is some ideas are not heard in the marketplace of ideas.

SLAPPs are filed most often by developers, and after them, by landfill owners and manufacturers. They tend to be based on one of six common torts: defamation (includes libel and slander), business torts (including interference with contract, business, and economic expectancy), judicial torts (includes abuse of process and malicious prosecution), conspiracy (joining with others to commit a tort), nuisance, and Constitutional or civil rights violations (includes due process, equal protection, and discrimination) (Canan and Pring 1988). Early research found defamation to be the most common grounds for filing (Canan 1989).

So what actions lead to SLAPPs? The answer is surprising. Triggers for SLAPPs include circulating a petition, writing to a government official, calling a consumer protection agency for assistance, speaking at a public meeting, and testifying at zoning hearings. SLAPPs are a vehicle used by corporations to prevent citizen participation, not lawsuits to be won. In fact corporations rarely win SLAPPs; if they do, a successful counter suit (a SLAPP-Back suit) often follows (Pell 1990). It seems that the goal of SLAPPs is to prevent people from exercising their political rights or to punish them if they do. Simply put, SLAPPs are a means to hamstring the opposition. The threat of a lawsuit is intimidating and enough to silence many people. As targets of a SLAPP can no longer speak in public on the issue, the discussion is relegated to the private arena of the courts. Overall, SLAPPs have a chilling

---

Box 4.1 *(Continued)*

---

effect on the marketplace of ideas. One lawsuit can have a ripple effect and result in any other opponents choosing to remain mute.

SLAPPs go for a short-term gain. Opposition is stopped long enough to complete a project, such as building a new housing development. The company may have to pay when the suit is lost and when a counter suit is won. But the objective was to buy time. SLAPPs are not the only overly aggressive tactic used to silence critics. Dezenhall Resources is a public relations firm run by Eric Dezenhall. This agency advocates and sells methods for silencing critics on the Internet. One popular idea of Dezenhall (2005) is "Stopping the attackers in today's assault culture." The firm vilifies any would-be critics, including the news media and activists. The aim is to stop the attacks. Not a bad idea in itself, but the tactics, including filing lawsuits and engaging in character assassinations, are questionable. For example, lawsuits are threatened in order to deter critics from hosting web sites or posting unfavorable comments about an organization. There may be extreme situations when critics' attacks are completely unfounded and such countermeasures are required. But these are the exceptions, and do not justify the general squashing of criticism under the rules proposed by Dezenhall Resources.

Enlightened corporations realize critics can provide insights into potential problems and ways to improve an organization. For example, activists have used the Internet to attack a number of Shell Oil policies. Shell Oil did not counterattack. Instead, it invited critics to make comments on the Shell web site. And people may say some very critical things to Shell's "face" this way. But the ideal of mutual influence means stakeholders must be allowed to try to influence organizations. Shell Oil gets this valuable point. Dezenhall and others of this ilk do not.

---

through which public relations affects society. This chapter is divided into three sections: issues management, social marketing, and a combination of the two. Issues management explores the public policy effects of public relations. Social marketing examines how public information campaigns shape society by altering behaviors. Finally, we consider how the two often overlap and coexist.

Public policy covers the legislative and regulatory rules devised by government bodies. Laws tell us how fast we can legally drive, what safety features manufacturers must include in our cars, and what information is placed on labels of food containers. *Social marketing* involves attempts to influence social behaviors related to health problems and risk behaviors. It covers a wide range of efforts designed to improve people's quality of life. We encounter social marketing in the public service announcements (PSAs) we see on television and in print or hear on the radio. Social marketing efforts have helped to reduce forest fires, to increase awareness of AIDS, and to encourage people to mentor children.

Issues Management: A Framework of Effects on Public Policy

Issues management is a discipline within public relations that was developed specifically to address public policy issues. The impetus is derived from corporations feeling the need for a more integrated and effective approach to shaping policy decisions. Issues management was created in the 1970s to meet that need. The interest in issues management extends beyond corporations. Organizations (any collective) have a need to be proactive, not reactive, in their interactions with the environment (elements outside of the organization itself). The environment can either impede an organization's ability to operate or facilitate it (Heath and Nelson 1986). Issues management is a process organizations can employ to prevent negative developments (problems) and to cultivate a favorable environment (opportunities).

Definitions of issues management tend to emphasize either the objectives or the process of issues management. The overriding objective in issues management is participation in the policy-making process (Chase 1977, 1980). Issues managers participate in the public policy process in order to influence the development of issues salient to their organizations. Issues are defined as "unsettled matters which are ready for decision" (Jones and Chase 1979: 11). By affecting the issue, the issues manager hopes to affect the public polices that emanate from it. The goal of this participation is to have the public policy question decided in a manner that is favorable to the issues manager.

A process definition of issues management lists the steps involved in the issues management process. The Chase–Jones Process Model, the most influential issues management model, has five steps: (1) issue identification, (2) issue analysis, (3) issue change strategy option, (4) issue action program, and (5) evaluation. Issue identification centers on detecting issues relevant to an organization. The issues manager scans the environment to locate emerging issues. Once located, an issues manager must predict the possible impact the issue might have on the organization. Issue analysis involves researching the issues in order to create a final prioritization. With research, an issues manager is better able to predict how the issue might impact on the organization. Using this impact assessment, a final prioritized list of issues is assembled. A prioritized list is necessary because issues managers can only address one or two issues at a time. The issue change strategy option centers on selecting the most feasible and practical strategy for responding. The issue action program involves communicating about the issue to various

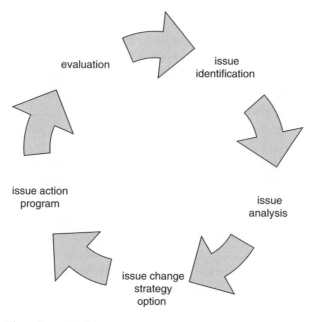

Figure 4.1   Chase–Jones Model

stakeholders. The stakeholders are sent messages tailored to their needs and through communication channels they utilize. Evaluation of the results is a matter of determining the effects of the issues management effort. Success is measured by how closely the actual outcome matches the intended outcome (Jones and Chase 1979).

The objectives and process definitions can be fused into a working definition of issues management. We define issues management as *the identification or creation of issues and the application of systematic procedures designed to influence the issue's resolution in a manner favorable to the issues manager.* This definition captures the two critical features of issues management. First, the definition identifies issues management as a specific set of principles. "Systematic procedures" implies that issues management has its own guiding tenets; it is not some unplanned venture. Second, the definition identifies the objective of issues management, the resolution of policy issues.

A weakness in the Chase–Jones Process Model is that it neglects how communication is utilized to manage issues/influence the policy making process. Crable and Vibbert (1985) extended the work of Jones and Chase with the Catalytic Model of issues management. The Catalytic Model it important because it focuses on the role of communication in influencing public policy. Communication is employed to create arousal. The Catalytic Model seeks to increase the number of people who are aware of the issue, accept the issue as a valid public concern (grant it legitimacy), and support the preferred policy option for resolving the issue. Communication is used to spread the word about the issue, create legitimacy, and win support for the policy proposal.

The Catalytic Model focuses on the status or importance an issue has for stakeholders, including policy makers. Influence on policy-making is a result of using communication to manage the status of the issue. An issue has five different status levels that reflect the life cycle of an issue: (1) potential, (2) imminent, (3) current, (4) critical, and (5) dormant. Communication is used to affect which status, or stage, an issue is at, and its importance for stakeholders (Crable and Vibbert 1985).

At the *potential* status, stakeholders begin to show interest in an issue. The key communicative action is to define the issue. The definition establishes the boundaries of the issue and can serve to attract or repel stakeholders to the issue. At the *imminent* status, additional stakeholders are beginning to accept the issue. An issue moves beyond the small circle

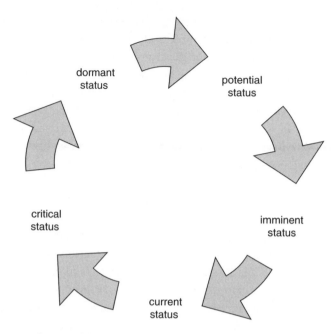

Figure 4.2   Catalytic Model

of people who created the issue. It builds legitimacy through endorsements and associations with history, tradition, or values. Legitimacy
messages help stakeholders to realize their connection to the issue and
accept that it is important to them. The issue is gaining power but is not
widely recognized in society (Crable and Vibbert 1985).

At the *current* status, the issue is circulated to a wide array of stakeholders. News media coverage or wide Internet exposure are used to
reach the current status. This status is marked by awareness of an issue
and the issues manager's side of the issue (the desired policy option). At
the *critical* status, there is pressure for a decision to be made. Issue
managers use persuasion to win support for their side of the issue (policy
option) and to pressure government agents into acting on the issue. Once
a decision is made, an issue is resolved and moves to the *dormant* status.
It is resolved for the time being. An issue remains dormant until someone or group recognizes its potential and attempts to revive it. But
interest can fade at any point, whatever status levels have been passed,
allowing the issue to slip into dormancy. Communication is a critical
factor for keeping people aroused and interested in the issue. However,

opponents of the issue can craft messages designed to create quiescence so that the issue fades away (Crable and Vibbert 1985).

The Catalytic Model is about the use of communication to influence agendas. By increasing awareness and legitimacy, issues managers can influence the public agenda (what people know about the issue) and the policy agenda (what the government will act upon). Public relations plays an active role in issues management and, therefore, in shaping society through policy decisions. A few case studies will illustrate how this can be done, and how public relations can be used either to create or to prevent change.

Issues management will involve conflicting views of how to resolve an issue. This means two or more people or groups can be trying to manage the same issue simultaneously. The news media will focus on the "lead" issues managers for the various sides. In fact, the various sides of an issue will be composed of coalitions. *Coalitions* are groups of people who come together to combine their efforts to influence the process and outcomes. As the Catalytic Model emphasizes, issues management is often a process of drawing various people and groups to one's own side of the issue. The existence of coalitions reflects the fact that in policy decisions there is power in numbers. As Heath (1997) notes, power is a function of the number of people supporting an issue. Hence, issues managers try to recruit allies and build coalitions (Heath 1997; Coombs 1998). For example, in the 1990s, the railroad and insurance industries joined forces to combat national legislation that would permit trucks to be three trailers long.

The remainder of this chapter presents brief case studies that illustrate this issues management process. They will focus on the primary issues managers. However, bear in mind that there were other forces at work in each of the cases.

EPA bans Alar under pressure

Until 1989, Uniroyal manufactured daminozide, a chemical that allows apples to stay on the trees longer. By staying on the trees longer, the apples looked better and were easier for growers to harvest. Daminozide was used for other fruits as well. The trade name for daminozide was Alar. In 1989, the Alar issue burst upon the scene. In a span of a few weeks Americans went from having no idea that Alar existed to demanding that the Environmental Protection Agency (EPA) ban its use. Alar was banned shortly after public relations efforts moved the issue to the front of the media, public, and policy agendas. The victory came with an unintended consequence that we will address at the end of the case.

Concern about Alar dates back to the 1970s. Early research indicated that when daminozide breaks down under heat, such as in processing fruits, a carcinogen is formed. Traces of Alar were found in samples of baby food and apple juice during the early 1980s. However, the EPA kept Alar on the market. There was an issue but not many people knew or cared about it. Enter the National Resource Defense Council (NRDC). The NRDC funded and released a study on daminozide titled "Intolerable risk: pesticides in our children's food." The report provided further evidence that daminozide can become a carcinogen when heated. Admittedly the levels have to be very high to pose a threat. Fenton Communications, a public relations firm, was hired by NRDC to help turn the public against Alar.

The key to the issue management effort was to make Americans aware of the risk, believe the risk was real, and pressure the EPA for change. Fenton Communications orchestrated a launch of the NRDC's report on February 26, 1989. *60 Minutes* featured a piece titled "A is for apple" on the link between Alar and cancer with a focus on the threat to children. Meryl Streep and other celebrities appeared on talk shows and spoke before Congress to testify about the dangers of Alar, especially for children. Children were at greater risk because of their smaller body weights and longer-term exposure to daminozide than adults. A grassroots groups known as Mothers and Others for Pesticides Limits was created to support the cause as well. A cancer threat to children was a huge news draw. Very rapidly people became aware of Alar, believed in its harmfulness, and wanted EPA action on it.

In March of 1989, the EPA banned the use of Alar. Uniroyal had already voluntarily ended production of the product. The banning was as much a response to public outrage as to the cancer threat. The EPA did not feel Alar was an immediate threat but said that it could pose a risk over time. Its announcement about Alar stated that the NRDC evidence did not provide definitive proof that Alar would hurt children immediately. In fact, the EPA encouraged people to continue eating apples that were exposed to Alar, although it admitted the concern: "In the last few weeks there has been a growing public controversy over the potential harmful effects of a chemical called Alar, which is used by apple growers to retain the crispness of their fruit as it goes to market" (Negin 1996). This statement seems to indicate that public pressure was the reason for the ban. The NRDC had executed a successful issues management effort. Alar had quickly gone through the critical, current, and – the problem having been resolved – into dormant status.

Issues have at least two sides. The apple industry opposed the NRDC efforts, and paid Hill and Knowlton one million dollars to mount a defense. But this public relations effort was "too little too late." The NRDC had captured the attention and minds of the American people. The apple growers filed a libel suit against the NRDC, CBS, and Fenton Communications. The case against them was dismissed in 1994. The Alar case then became a rallying cry for the food industry. News reports included stories about the Alar "scare" and Alar "hoax." The result was the development and passage of food disparagement laws in thirteen states. These are also known as "food libel laws" and were the grounds for the beef industry's 1998 lawsuit against Oprah Winfrey. The purpose is to prevent people from saying bad things about food that could then decrease sales of that food. In these states, people are limited in their efforts to raise concerns about food safety. Food safety groups won with Alar but the victory was costly because it provided the impetus for legislation that reduces the ability to raise food safety issues (Negin 1996). The Alar issue changed society far beyond the banning of a chemical. It has altered the manner in which many food safety issues must be publicly addressed. It's clear that public relations campaigns can have wide and unintended consequences.

AMA's objection to national health insurance

President Clinton was a champion of health insurance for all Americans. The issue was that millions of Americans have no health insurance and that hurts society. True to the Catalytic Model, national health insurance was not a new issue but one revived from dormancy. National health insurance began as an issue in the 1930s but never moved very far in the issues management process (Key 1964). It began to attract greater attention and legitimacy in 1948. In January of that year, President Truman called upon the country to adopt compulsory national health insurance. He felt national health insurance was necessary "to protect all our people equally against . . . ill-health" (Harris 1969: 36). Truman's re-election in 1948 was a sign of support for national health insurance.

Truman began his attempt to influence policy-making with his 1949 State of the Union Address. He restated the need for national health insurance. The poor were not receiving adequate health care because they lacked insurance. Truman outlined his plan in later speeches. National insurance would make sure all Americans had access to health care. The system would pay physicians but not make them employees of the state or interfere with how they treated patients. National health insurance was a way to insure proper health care for all Americans without infringing on the rights of physicians (Harris 1969). The Truman administration was trying to build awareness of and support for national health insurance. The President's messages made people aware of the issue, gave it legitimacy, and persuaded people to support it. Public opinion polls in 1948 showed 58 percent of the American people supported a national health insurance program. In 1949, Congressional mail ran 2.5 to 1 in support of the program (Starr 1982).

The American Medical Association (AMA) was not one of the groups swayed by President Truman's messages. The AMA decided to oppose Truman because the program could reduce physician autonomy. It asked each member to donate 25 dollars in order to build a war chest to fight national health insurance (AMA war chest, 1948). AMA viewed national health insurance as "socialized medicine"; they believed it was unnecessary and would reduce, not improve, the quality of health care in the US. The public relations firm of Whitaker & Baxter was hired to orchestrate the counterattack. The AMA would spend over one million dollars a year in its efforts to defeat national health insurance (Key 1964; Harris 1969).

The AMA campaign ran during 1949 and 1950. The typical public relations tactics were used: pamphlets, publicity through the news media, and speaking programs. The central message was that socialized medicine was evil. This perspective was presented at a time when socialism was a very negative term in the US (Burrow 1963). A successful link between socialism and national health insurance would sink the program. Citizens would be aroused to oppose rather than support it.

The pamphlets are a prime example of the socialized medicine angle. The most widely circulated pamphlet was "The voluntary way is the American way." It was fifteen pages long and followed a question and answer format. Here is a sample text:

Q. Who is for Compulsory Health Insurance?
A. The Federal Security Administration. The President. All who ser-
iously believe in a Socialistic State. Every leftwing organization in
America . . . The Communist Party.
Q. Would socialized medicine lead to socialization of other phases of
American life?
A. Lenin thought so. He declared: "Socialized medicine is the keystone
to the arch of the socialist state." (Starr 1982: 43–4)

Truth was not the issue. The quotation from Lenin has never been
found to exist. The purpose of the public relations tactic was to link
national health insurance to socialism.

The news media were willing to follow the publicity materials generated by the AMA effort. Press releases, "neutral" experts speaking on
the radio, and press conferences echoed that national health insurance
was socialized medicine (Paletz and Entman 1981; Starr 1982). The
neutral experts talked about socialized medicine and the media coverage
of the issue accepted the socialized medicine frame for national
health insurance (Harris 1969). The media agenda reflected the AMA's
desire to reject the national heath insurance proposal. A legion of
speakers was mobilized to address community opinion leaders directly.
A partial listing of the AMA speaking tour included 1,200 trade associations, 1,500 Kiwanis clubs, 4,500 Lions clubs, 2,300 Rotary clubs, and
9,000 YMCA city associations (Burrow 1963). The speakers program
served to amplify and reinforce the mediated messages about socialized
medicine.

We all know how the story ends. The US still has a problem with
people lacking health insurance. By the end of 1949, public opinion polls
found that only 39 percent favored national health insurance, well down
from the 58 percent just the year before. By 1950, Congressional mail had
shifted from support of the program to 4 to 1 against national health
insurance (Key 1964; Starr 1982). The public agenda had been influenced
to oppose national health insurance. The national health insurance
program was repeatedly voted down in Congress. The evidence suggests
that the AMA's success in labeling national health insurance as socialized
medicine significantly prevented the policy making process. Public relations was part of the reason the US did not adopt a national health
insurance program and still has not to this day.

Local battles: retailing and health care

The Los Angeles area is a very attractive retail market. Wal-Mart has been trying to strengthen its position there for a number of years. But it was dealt a blow in October 2002 when the City Council of Inglewood passed a ban on building large "box stores." The ban would not allow construction of a facility over 155,000 square feet that would sell over 20,000 non-taxable items like food. Wal-Mart supercenters are over 200,000 square feet and sell food. The ban was later rescinded under threat of a lawsuit. Wal-Mart, however, chose to avoid another battle with an unfriendly city council. Instead, it went to the people: it collected over 6,500 signatures in support of a ballot initiative, which would, if enough favorable votes were cast, allow Wal-Mart to build the super-center (Lucas 2004).

Wal-Mart spent over 1 million dollars on the campaign to win the vote, including in it extensive issue advertising. They were opposed by a number of groups, such as the United Food and Commercial Union, the Coalition for a Better Inglewood, and various religious organizations. One rally against the initiative featured the Reverend Jesse Jackson. In April of 2004 the ballot was held. It failed, with 39.3 percent voting "Yes" and 60.6 percent voting "No." Wal-Mart had lost this battle in the war to enter the Los Angeles area (Buckley 2004).

When we think of hospitals, we typically think of the area general hospital. It is a non-profit institution that provides a variety of services to the community. General hospitals face many burdens in delivering health care to the community. Of particular note is emergency care. Emergency rooms are costly to operate since many patients are under-insured or have no insurance. General hospitals balance the cost of emergency care with their other services, such as surgeries. Many outpatient surgeries are "profitable." The procedures can be performed for less than what insurance will pay. These "profits" are used to offset losses in areas such as emergency services and psychiatric care, and to provide community health outreach programs.

A Free-standing Ambulatory Surgery Center (FASC) is a growing kind of profitable health care service. FASCs are also known as "niche hospitals" and "surgicenters." They are operated by owner physicians, and provide only selected outpatient surgery and can be highly selective in their patients. By limiting themselves to surgical procedures that are profitable and patients that are fully insured, a FASC can turn in a nice profit for the investors. The problem is that general hospitals suffer when a FASC appears in town. The general hospital will suffer a drop in revenue as the "profitable" procedures are drawn away while they continue to absorb the cost of emergency care and treating the under-insured and uninsured. The result is often cuts in services provided, in community outreach, and in staff by the general hospital.

In 2003, Sarah Bush Lincoln Health System was faced with the prospect of a FASC opening near its facility in Mattoon, Illinois. Sarah Bush administrators knew they would be fighting a two-front battle. The first front was the Illinois Health Facilities Planning Board. This body regulates the building of new health care facilities to prevent over-providing health care to a geographic area. This battle would involve financial and health services analysis. The second front was the patient base of Sarah Bush. Sarah Bush was going to publicly oppose the building of the new FASC. However, local residents would be told by FASC supporters how this facility would provide competition, better care, and even lower health care costs. There would be a battle for local opinion.

The petition to build the FASC was known to Sarah Bush but would not become public until the official public hearing for the Illinois Health Facilities Planning Board was announced. That would be a three- to six-month time frame. Sarah Bush took the initiative of defining the issue early. The center was defined as a threat and not a benefit to local health care. It would exploit their advantage of selective patient care to drain money from Sarah Bush. In turn, Sarah Bush would be forced to end much of its extensive community outreach programs such as dental care for children. The well-documented negative effects of a FASC on general hospitals were used to support their definition of the situation. Employ-ees were briefed so that they could explain the issue to those who might ask about it. Sarah Bush used advertisements, direct mail, local speaking engagements, and newspaper interviews (the area has no local television stations) to explain the problems. Employees and community supporters wore maroon ribbons, the color of Sarah Bush. The local newspaper supported Sarah Bush in its opposition to the FASC.

A good sign for Sarah Bush was the actual public hearing. Anyone in the community could speak. Those speaking for the FASC were the physicians hoping to invest in the center. Those speaking for Sarah Bush were a "who's who" of local political, business, and community leaders. The news coverage and support for Sarah Bush suggest the hospital won the battle for community opinion. It won with the Illinois Health Facilities Planning Board as well. The Board ruled there was no need for an additional health care facility in the area. Public relations had played an important role in Sarah Bush's effort to defeat the FASC and to maintain the support of the local community.

Shaping Public Behavior

Public relations can be used to shape public behaviors and attitudes apart from the policy process. Most of these efforts are a form of social marketing. Underlying most social marketing is the process of moving people from awareness to action, much as in issues management. McGuire (1981) has identified six basic steps in social marketing: (1) presentation, target is exposed to the message; (2) attention, target pays attention to the message; (3) comprehension, target can understand the message; (4) yielding, the target accepts the message/attitude change; (5) retention, the target remembers the message; and (6) action, target engages in the desired behavior. This is a logical sequence. People are unlikely to change a behavior if they cannot remember why it should be changed. People are unlikely to remember a message if they disagree with it. People are unlikely to agree with a message if they do not understand it. People cannot understand a message they do not attend to and will not attend to a message unless they are exposed to it.

Unlike issues management, there typically are not "sides" in social marketing. People do not openly oppose most efforts designed to improve society. The opponents are individuals who are skilled at resisting persuasive messages. People can avoid them, ignore, misinterpret them, reject them, or choose not to change behaviors. For example, even with laws and campaigns, many people still do not wear seat belts. The challenge is to break through these defenses and develop the desired target behavior.

Kim Witte has refined our understanding of how social marketing messages shape behaviors by focusing on the area of health risk messages. Her extended parallel process model (EPPM) synthesizes fear appeal research to develop an effective means for using fear in persuasive messages. In fact most social marketing messages employ fear appeals, messages that arouse fear to induce compliance (Witte et al. 2001). People who receive a message make an appraisal about the threat and the efficacy of the recommendations (i.e. ways to address the threat). For the threat, people determine if the threat is relevant to them (whether they are susceptible to the risk) and whether or not it is significant (the risk is of significant harm). Why should they bother if the risk is unrelated to them or is insignificant? Perceived efficacy involves both response efficacy and self-efficacy. The belief that the requested behavior will work (be effective) is referred to as "response efficacy." "Self-efficacy" refers to the belief that they can perform the behavior. To be motivated to act, people must perceive both response efficacy and self-efficacy.

The appraisal of threat and efficacy results in one of three responses: (1) no response, (2) danger control response, or (3) fear control response. If the threat is irrelevant or minor, there is no response. If people decide the threat is relevant and significant, fear should move them to action. If people perceive response efficacy to be high, they accept the message and act to control the danger or risk; this is a "protection motivation response." In contrast, the defensive motivation response is a rejection of the message. In this case, people perceive that they themselves cannot prevent the danger (i.e. they have low self-efficacy), or doubt that acting as recommended would avert the threat in any case; they believe there is no use in controlling the danger. They might distort the message (i.e. use selective attention) or attempt to control their fear (the defensive motivation) by ignoring, denying, or discrediting the message (saying that it is trying to manipulate them) (Witte et al. 2001).

Campaigns to address social issues rely on some combination of education, engineering, and enforcement to succeed. Education is the most obvious part for public relations. Public information campaigns educate people about dangers and ways to remove those dangers from their lives. An example would be knowing that wearing a seat belt increases your chances of surviving an automobile accident. Engineering attempts to create an environment where people will face fewer risks. Air bags in cars are an example of engineering as are guardrails on highways. Finally, enforcement is composed of laws and regulations designed to protect people. Laws requiring the use of seat belts would be an example of enforcement. While recognizing any public information campaign mixes the three E's (education, engineering, and enforcement), we will focus on education because it most overtly entails public relations.

Keep America Beautiful

In 1953, volunteers formed the Keep America Beautiful organization in order to improve the appearance of local communities. In 1961, the Ad Council began working with the organization. It provided free expertise in developing social marketing campaigns (or public information campaigns). The Keep America Beautiful campaign focused on pollution. The idea was to create awareness of how litter and other pollution were damaging the environment and how individuals had a responsibility to help solve the problem. The campaign needed to combat negative attitudes and behaviors that led to pollution.

There was some success with the early "Suzy Spotless" messages. Suzy scolded people for littering. For two straight years the National Litter Index dropped. The big success was making the environment part of American values. By the 1980s, environmental concern was established as a societal value in the US. Much of the success of this social marketing effort is linked to the public service announcement (PSA) known as the "Crying Indian." (A PSA can appear in print, posters, or on radio, television, or the Internet.) This striking visual PSA, of a tearful Native American surveying the litter around him, increased the number of people aware of and concerned about littering. On Earth Day in 1971, a PSA featuring Native American actor Chief Iron Eyes Cody appeared for the first time. The tagline line was, "People start pollution. People can stop it." Iron Eyes Cody became synonymous with environmental concerns and Americans moved towards adopting a new value. The message was simple: do not litter. People could fall in line with that and the growing importance of the environment in general suggests that they continue to do so.

At the peak of the campaign, Keep America Beautiful reported receiving more than 2,000 letters a month from people wanting to take part in their local efforts. Keep America Beautiful reported that local teams had helped to reduce litter by as much as 88 percent in 300 communities, 38 states, and several countries. The success of the Iron Eyes Cody PSA for the anti-litter campaign led to hundreds of other environmental messages through the years under the Keep America Beautiful banner (Pollution, 2005). Of course the campaign also benefited from new anti-littering laws (enforcement) and the provision of more trash containers for motorists (engineering).

Keep America Beautiful's efforts followed McGuire's (1981) progression. The anti-litter messages were placed in various media outlets as PSAs and designed to catch the target's attention. The messages were easy to comprehend: if you don't litter pollution is reduced. Americans became aware that littering was contributing to pollution and seemed to accept that argument. Iron Eyes Cody helped to make the message memorable. Ultimately people did seem to change behaviors, since littering declined around the country. While successful, the campaign did not eliminate all littering. A campaign will only be effective for part of the target audience. No campaign can reach all of the people. Campaign planners must be satisfied with modest success rates.

Witte's work allows us to delve deeper into the success of Keep America Beautiful (Witte et al. 2001). For at least part of the target audience, litter and pollution did generate fear. The threat was relevant and significant. Moreover, the response efficacy was high. It is easy not to litter and not littering will help to reduce pollution. Hence, people in the target group did engage in protection motivation and did stop littering. Others in the target population kept littering. They could have deemed the threat minor or unimportant to them. Another explanation is that the litter bugs did not think the solution would work so they adopted a defensive motivation response. However we choose to analyze it, Keep America Beautiful did help to change American society by altering littering behaviors and helping to instill environmental concerns as a value in America. This success was a result of the public relations harnessed through social marketing.

Online sexual exploitation

It is shocking to think that children inside their own homes are not safe from distant sexual predators. The US Department of Justice estimates that one in five children has received unwanted sexual solicitation online. With over 24 million children online, the number involved is staggering. Since 2004, the Ad Council has worked with National Center for Missing and Exploited Children to raise awareness of the problem of online sexual exploitation. The campaign directs children and parents to www.cybertipline.com. This web site provides tips on how to detect, prevent, and report suspicious online behavior.

The dangers are very real. Joel Rensberger posed as an 18-year-old in a chatroom, by means of which he met a 13-year-old girl in Minneapolis, Minnesota. After talking to Joel by telephone, she agreed to meet him. In the police statement, the girl said Joel took her to a motel. He gave her a video game to play and some wine coolers, i.e. sweet alcoholic drinks. Joel raped her and then drove her home. Not all children live to tell of their abuse (Stadler, n.d.).

The campaign started by educating parents about the threat of online predators and how to protect their children. Parents did not realize the dangers their children faced online. A survey of parent Internet monitoring found that 51 percent did not have or did not know there was software for monitoring the online behavior of children. A full 95 percent did not understand the instant message lingo of their children. This meant they could not understand the messages they were monitoring (Parents' Internet monitoring survey, 2005). So a PSA was produced to educate parents by describing Internet lingo. In May of 2005 the focus expanded to include children. Part of this effort is the web site http://www.idthecreep.com. At this web site, children play a game designed to teach them about online predators. The screen says: "You think you know who is e-mailing, chatting, or IM'ing with you? Really? Can you tell who means well and who doesn't? Play ID the Creep and see how you score when it comes to picking out the bad from the good." The site mimics the communications that teenagers might encounter online in chatrooms, IM, or emails. The campaign against online sexual exploitation is still new. The campaign began by inducing awareness and is now moving towards behavior change. Parents are learning how to monitor the online behavior of children and teenagers are learning how to identify possible predators. The online site for teenagers provides a means of increasing efficacy. They can practice and learn how to detect possible predators, thereby increasing their confidence in knowing how to chat online safely. Actual analysis of the campaign is needed to gauge its effect but it has the qualities recommended by McGuire and by Witte.

Ready.gov: preparing for disasters

Have you visited the Ready.gov web site? Have you created a disaster plan and kit for your family? The US Department of Homeland Security thinks you have done all of the above actions. The campaign was launched in February 2003 with a series of print, radio, and television public service announcements. A new set of public service announcements was added in December of 2005 and the Ready Kids web site (www.ready.gov) was added in 2006 to teach children the value of preparedness.

The focus of the campaign is the Ready.gov web site, to which people are directed by public service announcements. Ready.gov is considered to be a comprehensive site for the information and tools needed for emergency preparedness. At the site, people learn the need for preparedness, how to construct a disaster kit, and how to make a disaster plan for their family. The focus was at first on families. From 2005, Ready.gov contained information about how to prepare businesses and communities for disasters. The centerpiece of the web site is the "Preparing makes sense. Get ready now" downloadable brochure. The brochure provides the information necessary to make a kit and create a plan. The campaign has a Spanish language component complete with its own web site, www.listo.gov (Emergency preparedness, 2006). The campaign focuses on general emergency preparedness and is not just terrorist specific. The preparation actions will help in case of fires or any natural disasters.

The Ready.gov campaign has had limited success. Research has found that the number of parents stocking supplies and making family communication plans has increased. However, the majority of American families still have taken no steps to prepare for an emergency (Emergency preparedness, 2006). The problem is not threat or efficacy. Americans do feel the need to be prepared, believe the actions will help, and that they can create plans and kits. When they visit the web site, they are very likely to make plans and kits. The flaw in the campaign seems to be attention. The Ready.gov public service announcements do not seem to be reaching people. The messages are being sent (presentation) but people do not seem to notice them (attention). Adults do not seem to know that Ready.gov exists. Ready Kids was created as a means of using children to reach their parents. A similar strategy was used to reach parents about recycling. Of course, preparedness is more complicated and threatening than recycling, so using children to reach parents may not be as effective. The government needs to find some way for the Ready.gov message to break through the clutter and reach American adults if the country is to become better prepared to cope with disasters.

Germany and social change

Nazi Germany offers examples of the extreme effect that public relations can have on a society. The Nazi government's PR was sometimes directed at benefiting its citizens, but its propaganda was in general employed without regard for the truth, and for immoral and horrifying ends. Clearly the Nazi Party, with its efficient propaganda machine, had greater influence on the people than they could have on the government. Although there is always the option of rebelling against, or at least not conforming with, a repressive government, any dissidence is unlikely to be effective. Adolf Hitler articulated his views of propaganda in *Mein Kampf*: "Its task is not to make an objective study of the truth . . . its task is to serve our own right, always and unflinchingly" (Hitler 1998). Messages were to be directed at the masses, emphasize emotions over logic, and be repetitive. This is not too far from modern views of advertising and how even public relations is sometimes practiced.

Nazi anti-Semitic communication

To win public support, the Nazi Party needed an enemy around which to rally the people. Joseph Goebbels was the primary architect of Nazi propaganda. He followed Hitler's direction to breed hatred for inferior races, especially the Jews. All manner of public communications were used to spread lies about "the Jew." To excite anger, Goebbels depicted the Jewish race as abominable, as the enemy of the German people, and the cause of their hardship. The Germans were targets of repeated messages that had no relation to reality, which were designed simply to instill emotions such as hatred and contempt. Demonizing a people makes it easier to accept their persecution and even their elimination. Nazi propaganda allowed the hounding, and later the killing, of Jews and other despised groups, to occur without widespread objection. Communication had been used poisonously to exploit prejudice and was entirely successful in influencing a society for the bad.

Nazi anti-tobacco campaign

Consider a place where cigarette advertising is banned, smoking prohibited in most public buildings, and a sophisticated anti-smoking public relations campaign is in place. This could be California or many other locations in the United States. In this case, however, we are talking about Nazi Germany (1933–45). The Nazi Party was motivated more by ideology than by a concern for the public health: a master race should not smoke. The government even funded studies that document some of the deleterious effects of smoking. Hence, public relations and threat of reprisal were used to reduce smoking in Nazi Germany.

A variety of public relations and regulatory tactics were utilized to influence Germans not to smoke. Popular health magazines, such as *Gesundes Volk* (*Healthy People: Journal for the Health and Entertainment of the Workforce*), contained warnings of the dangers of smoking. People saw posters that told of smoking's negative health consequences, and encountered anti-smoking messages in the workplace. The Hitler Youth and League of German Girls were used to spread the anti-smoking message as well. Regulations supported the cause. Smoking was banned in schools and some workplaces. And if someone had an accident while smoking, it was considered criminal negligence.

The anti-smoking campaign brings out the idea of mutual influence in public relations. People resisted the message and smoking rates continued to increase. They chose not to follow the messages of this public relations campaign. In part, the campaign's failure was due to its battling against people's strong desires and needs, as opposed to joining a battle already part-won. And in part the rejection of these attempts at influence can be seen as a small resistance to an authoritarian government. It was after all safer still to smoke or to start smoking than to oppose more central principles of the government (Hitler's anti-tobacco campaign, 2005).

Mixing Social and Policy Changes: Direct-to-Consumer Advertising and Big Pharm

For analytic purposes we have separated issues of management and social marketing, but clearly the two can overlap. Policy changes can affect society and social marketing can drive policy changes. Seat belts provide an excellent example. Social marketing and policies try to get us to buckle up. The topic of direct-to-consumer advertising in the pharmaceutical industry is an excellent illustration of how issues management and social marketing can become intertwined.

The United States and New Zealand are the only two major countries to allow pharmaceutical companies to advertise directly to consumers. Direct-to-consumer advertising (DTC) encompasses publicity efforts as well as advertisements (Moynihan and Cassels 2005). That is the connection between public relations and DTC. Public relations agencies such as the Chandler Chicco Agency specialize in health care public relations while large firms such as Edelman and Burston-Marsteller all have health care public relations as a specialty. Part of health care public relations is the promotion of pharmaceuticals. The success of a pharmaceutical launch is dependent on press coverage and "buzz" about the new medicine. Public relations firms carefully craft the media attention and buzz (Aziz 2004). In 2005 there was a major training event titled "Pharmaceutical Public Relations and Communications Summit," where pharmaceutical companies and public relations agencies could share ideas.

There is a plethora of evidence that DTC has impacted on society, in both good and bad ways (Angell 2004). On the positive side, DTC has empowered patients. Patients feel better informed about health issues and feel they have more choices for treatment. DTC messages raise awareness of disease and treatments. Both patients and physicians report that DTC leads people to consult a physician and request treatment, visits that frequently do result in treatment. Both also report that DTC facilitates patient–physician communication (C. Lewis 2003; Sheehan 2003). Ultimately DTC is helping people to realize they have a problem and to seek treatment for that problem.

On the negative side, DTC is helping to create new diseases, a concept known as *disease mongering*. Disease mongering occurs when non-medical problems become defined and treated as diseases (Mintzes et al. 2005). Otherwise healthy people are convinced they have a disease and must seek treatment. The severity and extent of the illness is exaggerated, partly through public-relations-generated news stories, in order to drive customers to a product. As Moynihan and Cassels observe, "With a little help from a headline-hungry media, the latest condition is routinely portrayed as widespread, severe, and above all, treatable with drugs" (2005: xiv). Public relations is a key element in efforts to create new diseases. In the language of public relations and marketing, conditions are being branded. The communication efforts might rename an old problem or identify an entirely new disorder (Moynihan and Cassels 2005).

Pharmaceutical companies are taking naturally occurring events, such as balding or erectile dysfunction, and creating a dire disease (Moynihan and Cassels 2005). Or problems that could be corrected through diet or life-style changes are instead cured through chemicals (Angell 2004). Disease mongering has been divided into four strategies: ordinary processes or ailments become medical problems (balding), mild symptoms are defined as markers of serious problems (irritable bowel syndrome), personal or social problems become medical concerns (shyness), and a naturally occurring risk becomes a disease (osteoporosis). A driving force in all four is the public relations aspect of DTC. News media coverage enlarges upon the advertisements to create greater awareness and fear of the "disease" (Moynihan et al. 2002).

DTC becomes a variety of social marketing that fits perfectly into Witte's EPPM model (Witte et al. 2001). The fear of the new disease becomes a motivator. People will become patients if they feel the disease affects them and is serious enough to warrant attention. If patients believe the media and advertisements, they ask for the medication because they believe the drug will work (response efficacy) and they are more able to take a medicine than make more complicated life-style changes (self-efficacy). Social marketing efforts purport to find problems and try to solve them. DTC, akin to the Catalytic Model, creates the disease and so the need to fight it. In reality, social marketing often creates or defines situations as problems that require attention. This is how DTC is in effect a form of social marketing.

Another negative aspect of DTC is the one-sided nature of the messages. Even with FDA regulations, DTC advertising still utilizes spin. The benefits of the drug are emphasized while the harmful side effects are downplayed. Against this, the FDA uses around only thirty people to evaluate around 2,000 DTC messages a year. Often a campaign ends before a complaint letter can be issued by the FDA (Angell 2004). Even the US government has recognized that this is problematic (GAO, 2000). The Vioxx problem brought the issue of risk and DTC to national attention. In 2004, the drug Vioxx was recalled because of a previously undetected negative side effect on the human heart. Millions of people had or were taking Vioxx when it was recalled. Consumers wanted to know why the risk was not known earlier and why the FDA had let this happen. This is where public relations, via issues management, is called upon.

Congress and the FDA were under public pressure to act. DTC has become an issue that various groups are trying to manage. How could pharmaceuticals be made safer? Both sides viewed DTC as a concern. Senator Bill Frist (Republican, Tennessee), a physician, issued a call in 2005 for no DTC to be done for the first two years of a new product. This time period would allow unknown risks to emerge before the drug went into wider circulation, for DTC does increase the prescription rate for a drug (C. Lewis 2003). The FDA began assessing the need for greater oversight and has proposed the development of the "Drug Watch" web site (Guidance, 2005). The web site would list any drug that the FDA is investigating for a serious side effect. As with Vioxx, a serious side effect often emerges after a drug is introduced to the market. Patients would then know when a medication was being investigated and what the side effects might be. In 2005, for instance, there were reports linking Viagra to a specific type of blindness (Reports of blindness, 2005). The argument is that patients need information when making decisions about medications. The Drug Watch site would offer another form of information to complement and perhaps counterbalance DTC messages. Only side effects that posed a significant health threat would appear on the Drug Watch site (Guidance, 2005).

Not surprisingly, the pharmaceutical industry was less than enthusiastic about the Drug Watch web site proposal. The industry line is that patients would not understand the information and be scared for no real reason. These are the same arguments critics level against DTC. Patients do not fully understand the information and they could be scared into seeking a medication. Underlying the reason to support DTC and the Drug Watch web site is the marketplace of ideas. Patients should be exposed to all relevant information when trying to make a decision.

The pharmaceutical industry has responded with a time-honored issues management technique: self-regulation. In August of 2005, PhRMA, the industry association for major pharmaceutical manufacturers, announced a new fifteen point "Guiding Principles" document for DTC. Most of the principles repeat existing FDA regulations such as that DTC information should be accurate and not misleading. New measures included educating physicians prior to a DTC campaign and excluding DTC messages in media targeted to age-inappropriate audiences (PhRMA Guiding Principles, 2005). Most of the major pharmaceutical companies publicly endorsed the plan. Below are some sample support messages.

PFIZER INC.

Pfizer Inc. strongly supports PhRMA's direct-to-consumer advertising principles. Pfizer is especially pleased with the unambiguous commitment of these principles to better meet patients' needs with improved communication of risks and benefits, which will enhance the industry's ongoing efforts to raise disease awareness, educate the public about prescription medicines and treatment options, and motivate patients to talk with their physicians regarding health concerns. (Pfizer Statement, 2005)

WYETH

Wyeth Pharmaceuticals, a division of Wyeth (NYSE:WYE), supports the Pharmaceutical Research and Manufacturers of America (PhRMA) Guiding Principles for direct-to-consumer advertising, which were unveiled at the American Legislative Exchange Council's 32nd Annual Meeting today in Dallas, TX.

"Like PhRMA, Wyeth believes that direct to consumer advertising provides value, particularly when it provides education about health care conditions and their treatment options and encourages dialogue between patients and their physicians," says Bernard Poussot, President, Wyeth Pharmaceuticals. (Wyeth support PhRMA, 2005)

Self-regulation is an issues management strategy. The idea is that if an industry regulates itself, there is no reason for the government to get involved. The pharmaceutical companies are fixing the DTC problems that Frist and the FDA are so concerned about. The self-regulations must be created and promoted through public relations. PhRMA had a media blitz with the new principles supported by the comments from its prominent members. The self-regulation is an attempt to prevent change to society. Only time will tell if the issues management effort will work. Oddly, the issue was created by the pharmaceutical industry itself through some abuses and unintended consequences of DTC. The social marketing of diseases prompted the call to regulate this activity.

Conclusion

In the first three chapters we focused on the microlevel of public relations with a focus on stakeholders and organizations. In this chapter we moved to a more macrolevel focus with a concentration on how public relations can be used to affect society (collections of stakeholders). Public relations does operate on different levels of influence. Some tactics try to influence relationships among stakeholders while others try to influence societal laws, values, or actions. Consider an activist group attempting to alter how an organization operates. The activist group can work with the organization to instill change, as described in the PETA and Burger King example (Chapter 3). Or it can use the government to force changes as in the case of the NRDC and Alar. Moreover, microlevel relationships are leveraged to create macrolevel changes. The web of relationships is used to build awareness of and concern for an issue or problem. Relationships between stakeholders are the raw material from which larger societal changes are constructed. Stakeholders influence others to recognize and support the issue or the need to address a social concern. In the next chapter we expand public relations' sphere of influence further with an analysis of the global level.

5

Global Effects of Public Relations

A significant trend since the 1990s has been the globalization of public relations. Public relations efforts often extend across national boundaries and the effects of corporation actions recognize no national borders (Starck and Kruckeberg 2003). The last chapter examined examples of public relations efforts designed to influence behavior and/or policy in individual countries. Public relations efforts now are often global in that they can affect stakeholders in many countries, both intentionally and unintentionally. Consider how colleges and universities in Canada, the United States, and Italy have joined in a campaign to change how Coca-Cola handles labor issues in Colombia. The activist group Killer Coke is engaged in an intentional action while Coca-Cola witnesses the unintended global effect of its labor relations in Colombia. Public relations messages designed in one country can affect stakeholders in other countries. The globalization of public relations is an extension of diplomacy, international activism, and international business. Stakeholder networks are now international and public relations operates in a much larger arena. In turn, the effects of public relations are international.

The corporate-centric view of public relations reproduced itself in global public relations. It is assumed that public relations went international only because corporations became multinational, and that global public relations emerged as a function of the growth of international business. However, global public relations is rooted in diplomacy and is as much a function of transnational activism as it is corporate life. Transnational activism recognizes that activist groups operate across national boundaries (Taylor 2005). A variety of names are used to label transnational activism including civil society, non-government organizations (NGOs), and private voluntary organizations (PVOs). We will explain shortly why we have chosen to focus on PVOs. In this chapter we discuss the development and implications of global public relations for governments, PVOs, and corporations. The way public relations is used to influence the relationship webs of these entities is explored through public diplomacy, transnational activism, and the unique demands of "going global."

Public Diplomacy: Government Public Relations Goes Global

Researchers have begun to articulate the relationship between diplomacy and public relations (e.g., Kunczik 1990; Signitzer and Coombs 1992; Manheim 1994). The relationship began with a realization of the overlap between the two fields. Diplomacy is a broad field defined as "the conduct of relations between states and other entities with standing in world politics by official agents and by peaceful means" (Sofer 1991: 65–6). Clearly the notion of relations offers a natural connection to public relations.

Public diplomacy is the sub-field of diplomacy with the strongest linkage to public relations (Signitzer and Coombs 1992). *Public diplomacy* can be defined as "attempts, either public or private, to influence public opinion abroad" (Manheim 1991: 90). The general target of public diplomacy is public opinion in another country: how stakeholders there feel about one's own country, or issue or action in it. Public diplomacy seeks to influence stakeholders in order to affect the behavior of the other country, particularly its foreign policy decisions (Manheim 1994). The boundaries are government or non-government organizations (NGOs) communicating to the people (the general population) of another country (Deibel and Roberts 1976; Signitzer and Coombs 1992; Manheim 1994). Formal diplomacy, government-to-government relations, is excluded from the definition. Public diplomacy is government-to-stakeholders. NGOs include political factions, corporations, and non-profit organizations. Hence, many entities may be involved in public diplomacy.

Public diplomacy provides a global arena for issues management and reputation management, two broad specialties within public relations.

Public diplomacy and issues management share a concern for influencing policy decisions. Public diplomacy is more restrictive in its approach than is issues management, and is limited to tactics that attempt to influence public opinion (e.g., publicity and advocacy advertising). Issues management is more expansive. In addition to influencing public opinion, issues management uses direct lobbying and grassroots lobbying to influence the opinions of the policy makers (Heath and Nelson 1986).

Through issues management, public diplomacy tries to influence policy decisions, foreign aid allotment, and foreign policy choices. Policy decisions lead to the laws and regulations created by a country. It is not uncommon for a business to have a stake in a policy decision being made in another country. Policy decisions such as tariffs, emigration, weapons sales, foreign aid, and embargoes have ramifications for many foreign interests outside of the country making the decisions. Foreign interests become issue managers as they try to shape public opinion about policy choices.

Historically, the term "civil society," or civil society organizations, was used to denote voluntary groups that are outside of the government but seek to manage issues and address social concerns. Civil society is a very broad concept encompassing non-government organizations, labor unions, neighborhood groups, faith-based organizations, professional associations, charitable organizations, and business lobbies to name a few (To serve and preserve, 2000; What is civil society?, 2006). Non-government organizations are a subset of civil society organizations that seek to address broad social issues and to help disadvantaged peoples and can include corporations (To serve and to preserve, 2000). Private voluntary organizations (PVOs) are a subset of NGOs that include only non-corporate entities. We will focus on PVOs because of their non-corporate focus.

Governments, corporations, and PVOs all attempt to manage issues in other countries. Collectively we will refer to these stakeholders as foreign interests. A good example would be tariffs on imported products. The EU has used tariffs on bananas to protect former colonies in Africa who now face competition from South American countries. Tariffs make a product less competitive in the marketplace because of increased prices. A government will want to support its own important industries, and so may try to persuade the importers of their products to reduce or abolish tariffs. Thus Ecuador constantly fights high EU banana tariffs (Ecuador rejects banana tariff proposal, 2005). Similarly, the US government has actively supported the efforts of American tobacco companies to move into Asian markets. A PVO might view tariffs as stifling development by restricting markets, and want to help exporters by opposing the tariffs that apply to them.

Reputation management concentrates on how stakeholders come to perceive an organization (Fombrun and van Riel 2004). Kunczik (1990, 1994) has detailed the concern countries demonstrate for the reputation, or image, they project in foreign countries. Mass media coverage is central to reputation cultivation (Kunczik 1990; Manheim 1994). In public relations, reputations are important to organizations because they affect how publics come to interact with the organization. The benefits of a positive image include increased investment and better employee retention (Dowling 2002; Davies et al. 2003; Alsop 2004; Fombrun and van Riel 2004). A country's reputation has a similar effect. A positive reputation can help to attract tourism, investment, and trade (Kunczik 1990, 1994), and serves as a resource for achieving other objectives. Foreign interests cultivate positive reputations in order to achieve tangible objectives related to decisions made by governments and other stakeholders, and in this media images are important. Both policy makers and citizens rely upon the mass media to formulate their opinions of foreign interests. The only group who would not rely so much on the news media would be policy makers who have direct experience of foreign affairs (Manheim 1994). Those lacking direct experience of the foreign interest will depend upon media coverage for their knowledge of it.

Foreign affairs are little known to most policy makers and citizens in the US. Both agenda setting and framing can help to explain the importance of reputation to tangible objectives. The media are especially effective in creating awareness for unobtrusive issues. Moreover, the media frame the information; they tell the general public how to interpret the very information they have revealed (Ryan 1991; Kosicki 1993). The media portrayal of a foreign interest tends to be *the* image received by most American people and policy makers. As a result, when a positive image is projected it can help to secure tangible rewards for the foreign interest in question. An invisible or negatively viewed country is unlikely to be rewarded by policy makers or decision-making individuals.

Foreign interests may wish to: (1) create awareness, (2) clarify a reputation, or (3) correct a reputation. Creating awareness simply makes publics aware of the foreign interest. There is only a passing recognition of a foreign interest and no clear mental picture or related evaluative features. Clarifying a reputation involves adding the detailed information publics need to create a mental picture and the related attitude. Correcting a reputation attempts to change the mental picture and attitude already held by the targets. An extended example will be used to illustrate these image objectives (Fisher 1970).

Benin is a developing nation. Developing nations are likely to receive very little media coverage in the western media. Therefore, the government of Benin might try to create awareness of Benin in selected western countries. It would then supply enough detailed information to create a reputation for itself in those western countries. However, what the western media tend to report about developing nations is the bad news, such as unrest and discord (Neuman 1996). Suppose Benin did have a series of protests. If the Benin government solved the problems causing the unrest it would have to put out more information to counteract the outdated image of turmoil.

Tangible objectives yield some kind of concrete result, either financial changes or a policy decision. Issues management pursues tangible assets in the political realm, often in the form of legislation or foreign aid. Tangible business objectives involve decisions made by non-government entities such as investors and suppliers. Business objectives include direct foreign investment, trade, and travel and tourism.

Direct foreign investment is money that foreign groups invest in a country, and is helpful in building a country's economic base. A country must have a visible image of political and economic stability before foreign capital is attracted to it (Aziz 1993). Trade involves increasing or maintaining exports. For our purposes, developing trade is restricted to attracting buyers and not the political side of trade and tariff negotiations. The travel and tourism industries attract visitors to a country. Tourists spend millions of dollars a year and are valuable assets to a country's economy. The primary decision-makers for direct foreign investment, trade, and travel and tourism are private business people and travelers, the decision-making citizens. These people decide where to invest, whom to buy from, and where to visit on vacation. Foreign investment is important because it is a far larger amount of money than foreign aid. Foreign interests compete to make direct foreign investment, and to partake in trade, and travel and tourism.

Public relations has significant implications for life beyond one's own society. Clearly various foreign interests are attempting to influence policy and business decisions in other countries. Foreign interests spend millions of dollars each year trying to influence the US government and citizenry through public diplomacy/public relations. Issues are managed and media coverage of countries is crafted (Manheim 1994).

Private Voluntary Organizations: Activism Goes Global

Activism has been global for well over two hundred years. Global activist groups are referred to as *private voluntary organizations* (PVOs). Other common terms include civil society organizations, citizen associations, and non-government organizations. We will use the term PVOs to separate activists from corporations, lobbyists, and industrial associations. Technically an NGO can include corporations and a civil society can include lobbying groups. PVOs, distinct from these latter groups, have a narrower focus and share a passion for advocacy. They take actions designed to make society better at the local, national, or global level; they promote social goals (Taylor 2005). There are thousands of PVOs in almost every location in the world addressing any issue you can think of and many you have never heard about. Some PVOs are only local in focus. On the global level, estimates place the number of PVOs at over 25,000. Amnesty International has over a million members with operations in over 90 countries. Well-known PVOs include, besides Amnesty International, Rainforest Action Network, Greenpeace, and Oxfam (Paul 2000).

PVOs cover a range of issues and topics. Reviewing a few of them will provide a flavor for their diversity. The Bretton Woods Project tries to influence the World Bank and International Monetary Fund (IMF). This PVO collects and shares information about the activities of these powerful economic entities. By sharing information and building coalitions, the Bretton Woods Project hopes to be a voice for greater transparency for the World Bank and IMF (About Bretton Woods, n.d.). The International Rivers Project seeks to aid local communities trying to protect their rivers and watersheds. It supports local efforts to preserve rivers and ecosystems that benefit humans and other biological communities (IRN, n.d.). Oxfam is a collection of 12 organizations working in over 100 countries to develop lasting solutions to poverty and suffering. The organization believes coalitions enhance power. Oxfam champions economic and social justice (About us, n.d.). Search for Common Ground is trying to change how the world approaches conflict. The focus is to shift conflict management from adversarial to cooperative approaches (Our Mission, n.d.).

PVOs are emerging as important actors in stakeholder networks, and are playing a larger role in international policy. They have been influential enough to help shape global agreements on such issues as the environment, women's rights, arms control, and the rights of children. PVOs were instrumental in the adoption of the Montreal Protocol on Substances Depleting the Ozone Layer of 1987 and the Mine Ban Treaty of 1997. They are often as important or more important than governments when it comes to making global policies. Even the United Nations views PVOs as an important legitimizing force in policy development (Paul 2000).

Corporations recognize the power and influence of PVOs as well, and international corporations are seeing their policies shaped by them. Often a PVO is engaged to create new policies in partnership with the corporation while at other times the PVO uses its power to influence corporate policies. PVOs draw heavily on their credibility. Edelman's Trust Barometer surveyed global opinion leaders about PVOs and corporations, including respondents from Europe, Latin America, Asia, and the United States. PVOs were generally the most trusted institutions, well ahead of corporations and governments – a reason for corporations to partner with PVOs. For instance, Wal-Mart has partnered with the Environment Defense Fund (EDF) to find ways to become more environmentally friendly. The first move by the EDF was to have Wal-Mart reduce packing waste for toys. As Taylor notes, "Partnerships between NGOs and business organizations are a win-win situation for both parties" (2005: 577). Other PVOs can leverage corporations into changing their practices. Greenpeace influenced Whirlpool to use environmentally friendly insulation while the Rainforest Action Network convinced Home Depot and Lowes not to buy products harvested from Canada's Great Bear rain forest. Richard Edelman, president of Edelman Public Relations is another who has observed that corporations are borrowing credibility from PVOs (Iritani 2005).

PVOs are built around managing mutually influential relationships. By leveraging their power, PVOs can alter the course of ships of commerce. They draw on a wide range of public relations tactics to inform, persuade, and activate stakeholders and corporations (Taylor 2005), including protests, web sites, e-mail alert systems, advocacy advertising, news releases, news conferences, and lobbying. PVOs are essentially public relations entities. These are the forms of communication that can influence corporations and governments.

PVOs often enter into coalitions to increase their power (Paul 2000). The Internet has made it easier for PVOs to link up with one another. This reflects the notion of "power in numbers" discussed in Chapter 4. Interconnected PVOs are referred to as *transnational advocacy networks* (TANs) (Keck and Sikkink 1998). Thirteen PVOs, including the Union of Concerned Scientists, Humane Society, Sierra Club, and the National Catholic Rural Life Conference formed a TAN to combat the overuse of antibiotics in producing food animals. The TAN targeted McDonald's, the world's largest buyer of food animals. It believed that if McDonald's said "no" to antibiotics, the animal producers would have to listen. McDonald's did indeed draft a "Global Policy on antibiotic use in food animals." The policy included a ban on the use of antibiotics in the poultry used by McDonald's (Greider 2003). A TAN had convinced one of the largest corporations in the world to change a significant business practice, again proving that PVOs can influence corporations.

TANs are further evidence of the global nature of activism. TANs erase national borders in the development of coalitions, selection of targets, and choice of issues. They demonstrate the public relations orientation and savvy of activists. It is through the exchange of information that TANs can form, and through these pooled power resources that they can persuade corporations or governments to change their behaviors and policies. When PVOs combine to form a more influential TAN (Keck and Sikkink 1998), the balance of power shifts to the benefit of the once marginalized PVOs. With this increase in numbers they find that corporations are more willing to listen.

Corporations: Increased Demands from a Global Network of Relationships

As stakeholder networks become global, the number of actors in the network increases. Refer back to Figure 3.1 and its depiction of the realistic stakeholder network, in which the corporation is linked to seven central actors: the suppliers, activists, media, government, community, investors, and customers. Each time the corporation goes into a country it has seven new actors to address. Each actor is actually a composite of many actors; there exist more than one government entity, community group, or media outlet in a stakeholder network. Now multiply this basic amount by the number of countries in which an organization operates. Imagine that the Y corporation operates in 25 countries. That would be 175 actors on the macrolevel. The number of actors in the network increases rapidly. Increases in numbers means increased demands from the stakeholders. And this increase will ultimately mean a greater chance of *conflict* between demands. The pressure to manage mutually influential relationships, public relations, intensifies for global corporations.

Corporate social responsibility offers an excellent example of the demands placed on global corporations. *Corporate social responsibility* rests on managing the relationship between a business and society. Howard Bowen, considered the "father of corporate social responsibility," recognized that organizations should operate in a manner consistent with the values and objectives of a society. This marks a point where corporations began to think beyond financial and legal responsibilities to ethical and philanthropic responsibilities (Carroll 1999). This shift in thinking required corporations to consider a wide range of stakeholders rather than simply privileging investors.

As Rawlins (2005) notes, organizations have responsibilities beyond the typical economic factors such as operating, paying taxes, and turning a profit. Stakeholders expect organizations to help solve social problems, not just produce wealth. Corporate social responsibility asks the question, "Is the organization a productive and positive member of society?" The answer takes into account how the organization impacts on a broad array of concerns ranging from human rights to the environment to sustainable development. Expectations for what constitutes corporate social responsibility vary greatly within and between different countries and stakeholders. In some locales it is enough to fulfill financial obligations. A shrinking number of stakeholders still believe the organization is socially responsible if it makes a profit for investors, employs local citizens, and pays taxes to the government. Financial interests alone may be enough to define the organization–society relationship. In contrast, in other locations socially responsible organizations must address worker rights, environmental impacts, wealth redistribution, and human rights in general, to be perceived as socially responsible. Social and environmental interests are used to define the organization–society relationship.

The UN Millennium Development Goals illustrate the varied views of corporate social responsibility. Can you recall any of the eight goals? Did you know there were eight goals? Had you ever heard of the UN Millennium Development Goals before? The eight UN Millennium Development Goals are:

1   Eradicate extreme poverty and hunger.
2   Achieve universal primary education.
3   Promote gender equality and empower women.
4   Reduce child mortality.
5   Improve maternal health.
6   Combat HIV/AIDS, malaria, and other diseases.
7   Ensure environmental sustainability.
8   Develop a global partnership for development.

The UN Millennium Development Goals were adopted in 2000, so they are not new. However, few US companies discuss the UN Millennium Development Goals when detailing their socially responsible actions. In contrast, such discussions can be found in the writings of some UK corporations. Unilever, for example, has a report on its web site that documents its efforts in Indonesia that relate to the UN Millennium Development Goals. The report was written by Oxfam, a PVO, in cooperation with Unilever, so it is an evaluation by an outside agency, not Unilever's interpretation of its progress on social issues (Exploring the links, 2005).

Some corporations and PVOs are even talking about corporate social opportunities (CSO). A CSO could consist of making sustainable products and services available to low-income people in developing countries. One variant of CSO is to develop smaller packages of products that low-income people can afford. Unilever has created sachets, smaller packages, of basic goods such as tea, laundry soap, and hand soap (Unilever, 2005). The concept of CSO provides yet another definition and set of expectations relevant to corporate social responsibility.

Public relations is a crucial element in addressing corporate social responsibility. Organizations must listen to, inform, and influence stakeholders through PR if they are to be perceived as socially responsible. We will focus on the role of mutual influence in the development of corporate social responsibility to illustrate pressures faced by global corporations.

Some writers equate social responsibility with a license to operate. If the organization is deemed legitimate it is allowed to operate (Going global, 2005). Being labeled as socially *irresponsible* can lead to an organization losing that license through some combination of strikes, sabotage, protests, boycotts, negative media coverage, or political action. More bluntly, stakeholders can exercise their influence in the stakeholder network with the objective of ending or amending the organization's license to operate. Stakeholders can define what constitutes being a good corporate citizen for a multinational organization. Table 5.1 lists some of the expectations organizations will encounter around the world.

PepsiCo's eventual exit from Myanmar illustrates global concerns about their license to operate. In 1993, social activists began protesting PepsiCo's operation of facilities in Myanmar. The activists' position was that revenues from PepsiCo operations helped to fund the SLORC government and its violation of human rights. Through the use of the Internet and the media, the NGO known as "Free Burma Coalition" raised awareness of PepsiCo in Myanmar. Soon the investors and some large customers, most notably Harvard University, joined the activists in calls for PepsiCo to leave Myanmar. Stakeholders were coalescing in the network to pressure PepsiCo to change, and in 1997 PepsiCo severed all ties with Myanmar. Stakeholder pressure was the primary reason for this business decision. Stakeholders redefined operating in Myanmar as

Table 5.1 Expectations of organizations

1 Create employment.
2 Make products affordable and accessible.
3 Encourage good government.
4 Uphold basic international rights.
5 Improve access to education and health care.
6 Do not harm the environment.
7 Protect workers from harm.
8 Reduce poverty and inequity.
9 Increase revenues for local areas.

socially irresponsible. This redefinition was the reason for Levi Strauss and Liz Claiborne leaving Myanmar as well (Cooper 1997; Coombs 1998). Stakeholders had shown that they could influence corporate global actions.

In 1995, Shell Oil was to decommission the Brent Spar oil buoy, which was located in the North Sea. Shell went through all the formal channels with the government of the United Kingdom. The result was an agreement to tow the Brent Spar to a specified location and sink it in deep water. However, Greenpeace did not agree with the action, fearing the many pollutants contained in the Brent Spar. Before Shell could sink the Brent Spar, Greenpeace activists boarded and took up residence. With people on board, Shell Oil could not sink the buoy. As noted in the discussion of issues management, various groups will be involved with the different aspects of an issue. There were many other players beyond Shell Oil and Greenpeace who had a stake in whether the oil buoy was sunk or brought to shore for disposal. Someone, but not Greenpeace, would make money by securing the contract to dispose of the oil buoy. However, Greenpeace and Shell Oil were the most visible protagonists in this drama. For Greenpeace, that visibility was a result of their public relations efforts to promote the need for on-shore disposal.

Fortunately for Greenpeace, the UK has a much gentler approach to activists than the French. The French government had organized the sinking of a Greenpeace ship in the 1970s, in New Zealand, for interfering with nuclear tests. Greenpeace posted material about the Brent Spar and the ongoing situation to a web site, and gathered strong support in Europe and other parts of the world. In turn, a dialogue between Greenpeace and Shell Oil was opened. The UK government withdrew the permit and eventually Shell Oil towed the Brent Spar to shore for decommissioning (Heath 1998). Again, activists used communication to leverage influence and alter corporate behavior.

As the PepsiCo and Brent Spar cases illustrate, problems arise when there are gaps between what stakeholders expect an organization to do to be socially responsible and what an organization actually does. There are two types of gaps, perception and reality. Perception gaps exist when an organization has changed policies to meet expectations but those changes have not been communicated to stakeholders. Stakeholders keep pressing on what organizational management views as an old issue. Research in the United Kingdom has found that organizations do a rather poor job of communicating their socially responsible actions to stakeholders (S. Lewis 2003). Public relations can be used to communicate the changes and bridge the perceptual gap.

A reality gap occurs when organizational policies do not meet stakeholder expectations. It is a real risk for an organization and must be managed before it damages the organization. Allowed to fester, a reality gap will lead stakeholders to use their influence to force change on the organization, possibly through government regulation or legislation. As noted in Chapter 4, organizations prefer voluntary changes to mandated ones. Hence, management would prefer to find and address the gaps without government intervention or further stakeholder pressures.

In 2005, Robert Mugabe's repressive government in Zimbabwe expanded its program of farmland repossession and abuses of human rights. In a manner reminiscent of the Myanmar situation, stakeholders began to demand corporate attention to this issue. More precisely, corporations were encouraged not to conduct business with farms that had been seized illegally. Supermarkets and flower stores were at the center of the Zimbabwe storm. Produce and flowers were being purchased from farms that had been illegally seized or used by the government to generate revenues. The argument was about such trade being used to support a repressive government.

The controversy was especially keen in the United Kingdom. Larger retailers in the UK are signatories to the Ethical Training Initiative (ETI). Table 5.2 outlines some of the basic ideas behind the ETI. The ETI initiative concentrates on policing global supply chains. Organizations are to insure the people who supply them are respecting human and labor rights. This is similar to the garment industries' efforts to end the use of child labor and sweatshop conditions from its suppliers. Activists urged UK supermarkets to follow ETI and to insure the farms they used in Zimbabwe were not illegal or government proxies. Corporations can turn to third-party auditors such as Justice for Agriculture (JAG) for help. JAG is a Zimbabwean organization that verifies the legality and working condition of farms in that country. Tesco, a major supermarket chain in the UK, stopped importing from two farms in Zimbabwe after ownership changed. Tesco management felt they could no longer guarantee that those farms met ETI standards (Hall 2005). Stakeholder expectations were again shaping corporate behavior. The Zimbabwe example demonstrates how changes in geo-politics can impact corporate actions.

Table 5.2   Ethical training initiative base code

1	Employment is freely chosen.

1.1	There is no forced, bonded, or involuntary prison labour.
1.2	Workers are not required to lodge "deposits" or their identity papers with their employer and are free to leave their employer after reasonable notice.

2	Freedom of association and the right to collective bargaining are respected.

2.1	Workers, without distinction, have the right to join or form trade unions of their own choosing and to bargain collectively.
2.2	The employer adopts an open attitude towards the activities of trade unions and their organisational activities.
2.3	Workers' representatives are not discriminated against and have access to carry out their representative functions in the workplace.
2.4	Where the right to freedom of association and collective bargaining is restricted under law, the employer facilitates, and does not hinder, the development of parallel means for independent and free association and bargaining.

3	Working conditions are safe and hygienic.

3.1	A safe and hygienic working environment shall be provided, bearing in mind the prevailing knowledge of the industry and of any specific hazards. Adequate steps shall be taken to prevent accidents and injury to health arising out of, associated with, or occurring in the course of work, by minimising, so far as is reasonably practicable, the causes of hazards inherent in the working environment.
3.2	Workers shall receive regular and recorded health and safety training, and such training shall be repeated for new or reassigned workers.
3.3	Access to clean toilet facilities and to potable water, and, if appropriate, sanitary facilities for food storage shall be provided.
3.4	Accommodation, where provided, shall be clean, safe, and meet the basic needs of the workers.
3.5	The company observing the code shall assign responsibility for health and safety to a senior management representative.

4	Child labour shall not be used.

4.1	There shall be no new recruitment of child labour.
4.2	Companies shall develop or participate in and contribute to policies and programmes which provide for the transition of any child found to be performing child labour to enable her or him to attend and remain in quality education until no longer a child; "child" and "child labour" being defined in the appendices.

(Continued)

Table 5.2 (Continued)

4.3	Children and young persons under 18 shall not be employed at night or in hazardous conditions.
4.4	These policies and procedures shall conform to the provisions of the relevant ILO standards.

5	Living wages are paid.

5.1	Wages and benefits paid for a standard working week meet, at a minimum, national legal standards or industry benchmark standards, whichever is higher. In any event wages should always be enough to meet basic needs and to provide some discretionary income.
5.2	All workers shall be provided with written and understandable information about their employment conditions in respect to wages before they enter employment and about the particulars of their wages for the pay period concerned each time that they are paid.
5.3	Deductions from wages as a disciplinary measure shall not be permitted nor shall any deductions from wages not provided for by national law be permitted without the expressed permission of the worker concerned. All disciplinary measures should be recorded.

6	Working hours are not excessive.

6.1	Working hours comply with national laws and benchmark industry standards, whichever affords greater protection.
6.2	In any event, workers shall not on a regular basis be required to work in excess of 48 hours per week and shall be provided with at least one day off for every 7 day period on average. Overtime shall be voluntary, shall not exceed 12 hours per week, shall not be demanded on a regular basis and shall always be compensated at a premium rate.

7	No discrimination is practised.

7.1	There is no discrimination in hiring, compensation, access to training, promotion, termination, or retirement based on race, caste, national origin, religion, age, disability, gender, marital status, sexual orientation, union membership, or political affiliation.

8	Regular employment is provided.

8.1	To every extent possible work performed must be on the basis of recognised employment relationship established through national law and practice.

(Continued)

Table 5.2 (Continued)

8.2	Obligations to employees under labour or social security laws and regulations arising from the regular employment relationship shall not be avoided through the use of labour-only contracting, sub-contracting, or home-working arrangements, or through apprenticeship schemes where there is no real intent to impart skills or provide regular employment, nor shall any such obligations be avoided through the excessive use of fixed-term contracts of employment.
9	No harsh or inhumane treatment is allowed.
9.1	Physical abuse or discipline, the threat of physical abuse, sexual or other harassment, and verbal abuse or other forms of intimidation shall be prohibited.

Public relations is well positioned to address the reality gap. First, to find the gap an organization must listen to its stakeholders. As noted in Chapter 2, public relations is a boundary-spanning role that should convey stakeholder concerns to management. Public relations is a matter of listening to stakeholders and representing their interests to management. Forward thinking companies anticipate gaps and work to prevent them. Public relations can be used to make stakeholders aware of what an organization is doing to meet potential problems before they grow to serious proportions. Chiquita and FedEx can illustrate the prevention of gaps.

Chiquita is one of the largest banana growers and sellers in the world. Since 1992, it has been part of the Rainforest Alliance's Better Banana Project. The Better Banana Project tackles a variety of social and environment issues related to Latin America banana farms, such as the environmental impact of farming practices. By 2000, Chiquita had reached Rainforest Alliance certification on 100 percent of its Latin American banana farms. As a result of the Better Banana Program, Chiquita also sells Rainforest Alliance certified bananas in nine European countries. In 2003, Cyrus Freiheim, the chairman and chief executive officer of Chiquita, stated: "Adopting the Rainforest Alliance standard had been one of the smartest decisions Chiquita has ever made. Not only have we helped the environment and our workers – through better training and equipment – but we also learned that profound cultural change is possible" (Corporate Conscience, 2003).

Odds are you never heard of the Better Banana Project or thought much about banana farming practices in Latin American. The Rainforest

Alliance and other activist groups have been thinking about it since the early 1990s. As a major banana seller, Chiquita knew this concern could grow and eventually become a reality gap. Through public relations, Chiquita informed stakeholders globally about its practices. News releases and web site posting by Chiquita and by the Rainforest Alliance were used to spread the message. Chiquita had changed practices and used public relations to communicate its actions and prevented an expectation gap.

FedEx delivers packages around the world and was featured in the Tom Hanks' movie *Castaway*. The FedEx trucks, well known in many places, consume fuel and create problematic emissions. In 2000, Environmental Defense asked FedEx if it would be interested in a plan to reduce the amount of fuel consumed and emissions created by its delivery fleet. FedEx joined with Environmental Defense a few months later in a partnership called the Future Vehicle Project. The goal of the partnership was to develop fuel-efficient, low pollution delivery vehicles. More specifically, the trucks were intended to increase fuel efficiency by 57 percent, reduce smoke-causing nitrogen oxide emissions by 65 percent, and reduce particulate emissions by 96 percent (FedEx expands, 2004).

Over the next four years, the Future Vehicle Project worked with truck manufacturers to design, build, and test hybrid electric delivery trucks. The hybrids are ideal for the stop-and-go driving of delivery trucks. In February 2004, the first Eaton Corporation hybrid trucks began deliveries in Sacramento, CA. By the end of the year, 20 hybrid electric trucks were in the FedEx fleet. This is a small step, but by 2015 the entire 30,000 truck fleet will consist of hybrids (Getting in gear, 2005).

As with Chiquita and the Rainforest Alliance, the public relations effort was a partnership as well. Both Environmental Defense and FedEx issued news releases as the project progressed and had pages on their web sites devoted to the Future Vehicle Project. Corporations benefit from third-party endorsements, non-corporate entities making positive comments about the organization. Thus, the public relations messages created by the activist partners were valuable to both Chiquita and FedEx. Stakeholders are more likely to respond favorably to these socially responsible actions when the actions are endorsed and messages sent by activists. A potential expectation gap was averted. Chiquita and FedEx will be remembered as pioneers in their industries. Each had become a leader on a social issue of critical importance in their respective industries. Contrast this to being viewed as a corporation that failed to meet its obligations to a social issue. Being a leader on a social issue is much more beneficial than being an object of scorn for failing to be a good steward. PepsiCo and Shell Oil would be glad of reputations as good as Chiquita's and FedEx's.

In addition to helping prevent an expectation gap, public relations can create an awareness of them in the first place. Both the PepsiCo and Shell Oil cases illustrate how public relations can create expectation gaps and the pressure to resolve those gaps. How those gaps are resolved is another question.

One option for narrowing expectation gaps is to change organizational behaviors. PepsiCo, Levi Strauss, and Liz Claiborne all left Myanmar. Major pharmaceutical companies voluntarily changed rules for the use of direct-to-consumer (DTC) advertising in an effort to be more responsible in the use of promotion tactics. The changes reflect public concern over the FDA not being able to fully review DTC advertisements before they are presented to consumers (Sheehan 2003). In the case of Shell Oil and the Brent Spar oil buoy, the organization followed the desires of the activist stakeholders. The Brent Spar was towed to port and dismantled on shore rather than sunk to the floor of the North Sea (Heath 1998). Public relations is important in explaining to stakeholders whether their expectations will be met fully, or to a small extent, or not at all. An organization cannot meet all expectations, And different stakeholder groups can hold different and conflicting expectations. Management should be honest and, when it is not going to address an expectation, should admit it and say why it chooses not to. The same holds true when the gap can be narrowed only slightly. Public relations can help to prevent stakeholders from developing false expectations. By explaining why a gap will still exist, public relations can facilitate understanding between the organization and the stakeholders. Stakeholders may not like the outcome but will understand what was done and why, and will see that the organization may have legitimate reasons for not meeting expectations. These expectations might be unrealistic at that time, for instance. By communicating the reasoning, the organization may reduce the animosity inherent in an expectation gap. In sum, by engaging stakeholders, it can learn about, address, or modify expectations.

Expectation gap complications

The ability to address expectation gaps is complicated by competing voices and by organizational interests. Each of these two factors can result in an expectation remaining unfulfilled and the organization not having a very satisfying rationale for allowing the expectation gap to exist.

As noted earlier in the chapter, global organizations face a multitude of expectations. There are many stakeholders attempting to influence how the organization operates. Power once again plays a vital role in who is heard and gains influence. Power is never equally distributed among stakeholders, a point we have touched on many times in this book. Powerful stakeholders find it easier to express opinions and to be heard; they can more effectively engage in influence. This can even mean competition among activists and community groups. Large PVOs have greater influence than local community activists. The PVOs have enough power to speak directly to headquarters. Local community groups must rely on local management relaying their concerns to headquarters. Even activist groups can use power to silence another's voice (Going global, 2005).

Power reduces the distance to headquarters and increases the influence. In the stakeholder network, the loudest voice has the most power and greatest ability to influence. It is easier to ignore the marginalized stakeholders because their slight influence will result in minimal damage to an organization in comparison to powerful stakeholders. We might ask if it is ethical to ignore powerless stakeholders. In most instances it is not illegal and the consequences are often positive for the organization and most of its stakeholders. However, if we subscribe to the ethic of care, ignoring stakeholders is unethical. An organization must be concerned with the welfare of all of its stakeholders. All interests must be considered. This does not mean you please all of the stakeholders all of the time but you are aware of the consequences of your actions and attempt to minimize the harm that can result from those actions.

Another reason for expectation gaps is that the concern does not fit with organizational interests. Many organizations operate corporate social responsibility on the basis of what is good for business. The organization will only address social and environmental issues that will somehow help its financial performance (Going global, 2005). For example, organizations often invest in local education and health care. Improved education can create a better labor pool while better health care can keep workers healthy and more productive. Reasons to address expectations from a business point of view would include increasing productivity, reducing litigation, reducing production costs, or improving marketing efforts. The business angle reflects the powerful voice of investors in the stakeholder network. Consider the example of the construction company faced with anti-road protestors. The corporation's position was that it only builds the roads; it does not make road policy. One executive wondered if they would build gas chambers if paid to do so. The answer was no, but that roads were not gas chambers so they would move forward on the profitable project. The business case out-weighed the activists' concerns. Generally, management does not want to face the wrath of unhappy stakeholders, so expectations that do not address business interests are set aside. This may not sit well with some stakeholders because what they feel to be important may not mesh with the company priorities. The business case can set the stage for confrontations over expectations.

We believe it is a mistake to think corporate social responsibility is easily measured in financial gain or that it should be measured that way. The values case is that organizations should address expectations that are morally right (Going global, 2005). From about 1994 the Body Shop agitated about the imprisonment of twenty Nigerian dissidents because Anita Roddick, then CEO, believed it was the right thing to do. Roddick and the Body Shop supported a letter-writing campaign designed to have the dissidents freed. Posters were placed in the windows of Body Shop stores around the world. The signs remained in US malls even when mall officials expressed displeasure with the political statement. Roddick also helped to organize demonstrations, cultural events, and lobby politicians. After five years, nineteen dissidents were freed. The twentieth, Ken Saro-Wiwa, was executed two years into the campaign (Weelwright 2001). As Roddick stated, "If big business is more powerful than governments and does not care about human rights, then God help us all" (Marlowe 1998: 12). A value call, not a business call, had led the Body Shop to seek the freedom of the dissidents.

On the dark side of the Nigerian controversy was Shell Oil. Shell Oil is a major operator of oil wells in the Ogoni region of Nigeria. The dissidents were jailed for protesting at the exploitation and environmental damage the oil drilling was inflicting on their people. The oil came from Ogani land but the profits were not being shared with the poverty-stricken people in the region. The Nigeria government even engaged in a form of ethnic cleansing to eliminate opposition. Protest and violence mark the Ogani oil fields to this day. Shell Oil was viewed as a key supporter of the brutal Nigerian government. Activists and Anita Roddick challenged Shell Oil to use its influence to help the Ogani people (Roddick 1996). For years Shell Oil was deaf to such calls but did eventually learn to be more sensitive and responsive to stakeholder concerns.

Through the Brent Spar and Ogani issues, Shell Oil has come to appreciate the influence of stakeholders and the need to understand and to address their reasonable expectations (Donkin 1997). Shell Oil now recognizes society as one of its key constituents, along with share-holders/investors, customers, employees, and suppliers. Shell has a very open communication policy with stakeholders now. A unique public relations tactics is the web site Tell Shell. Shell Oil provides this forum for people to post messages about Shell and its policies. Most of the posts are critical of Shell Oil. Some sample negative comments posted at Tell Shell include "BOYCOTT SHELL!! FREE THE ROSSPORT FIVE" and "I am appauled [sic] at Shell's bully boy tactics in Ireland, which reveal the lie behind their 'good neighbour' rhetoric" (Tell Shell, 2005). Shell Oil clearly has some stakeholders upset about the pipeline and impri-soned protestors in Mayo, Ireland. And those stakeholders are not just located in Ireland. Time will tell how these stakeholders might influence Shell Oil. Still, the forum gives people a voice and Shell management a chance to hear.

The Tell Shell forum gives critics a mechanism for reaching Shell Oil. Of course how responsive Shell Oil really is seems to be a point of contention at Tell Shell. However, few corporations provide a public space for critics and the potential to hear them first hand. Part of mutual influence is understanding the parties you are attempting to influence. Shell Oil is using public relations to listen to stakeholders, find expect-ations gaps, and, in some cases, address those problems early instead of waiting for another public outcry.

Ethically, an organization must try to understand the values and concerns of its stakeholders. Part of an ethic of care is to avoid indiffer-ence. Not understanding the values and concerns of stakeholders is a clear sign of indifference. Appreciating values shows respect and helps to build connections. Still, values can conflict and there is no guarantee the organization and stakeholders will agree on all values. Regardless of the model of corporate social responsibility an organization employs, there is room for expectation gaps to exist and linger. Once more public relations can help by explaining why the expectation gap exists and will remain. This does not mean stakeholders will embrace the message but at least each side knows where the other stands and why. This provides hope of mutual understanding and perhaps cooperation. Stakeholders and organizations work together to determine what standards are appropriate for judging corporate social responsibility. This is an example of what Botan and Taylor (2004) refer to as the *co-creation perspective*. In other words, stakeholders are partners in the process of defining what corporate social responsibility means.

Conclusion

We live in a highly interconnected world. Policy decisions by governments, PVOs, or corporations in one country can impact on the lives of people in other countries. Consider the movement of call centers from the US to India and other parts of Asia. Some cities see lost revenues while others reap the benefits of employment and new taxes. Public relations is a factor in this interconnected world. Stakeholder networks know no borders. The government of Spain uses a web site to bring US tourists to its shores. Concern over land seizures in Zimbabwe result in a UK supermarket chain changing suppliers to meet stakeholder expectations. The Body Shop fights to post political statements in US stores in order to help political prisoners in Nigeria. Shell Oil alters plans for the Brent Spar oil buoy because Greenpeace takes its cause worldwide via the Internet. Governments, activists, and corporations can use public relations to influence decisions and lives in other countries. The extent of that influence depends upon the power and skill of actors utilizing public relations.

Early in this book we considered some of the harsh critics of public relations. A common refrain was that public relations was too powerful. It hid in shadows manipulating how we thought and acted. Public relations is not as all powerful as its critics would have us believe.

However, through its efforts to exercise influence, public relations does have an effect on people's lives. We have tried to demonstrate how public relations has been used to create both positive and negative outcomes for people. Public relations is much like the law; some will use it to hurt others while others will use it to benefit society. It is misguided to assume that public relations is inherently unethical or inherently ethical. Ultimately public relations is as ethical as the people employing it.

Whether we like it or not people will continue attempts to manage mutual influence. Public relations is a natural and necessary function in society. What is important to understand is how public relations can shape our lives. Knowledge is power. By understanding how public relations works we are better able to resist those efforts when need be and to use those same tactics to improve the quality of life for ourselves and others.

Where We Have Been

We started this book by wondering if society really needs public relations. The answer is still "yes." Public relations plays a vital role in building and maintaining the networks of stakeholders and organizations that make society possible. The connections and corresponding social capital allow these various actors depicted in Figure 3.1 to engage in mutual influence. This engagement naturally will be a mix of conflict and cooperation.

The parable of the blind men and the elephant is found in writings from ancient China and India. The parable involves six blind men led to meet an elephant. Each feels a different part of the great beast. The men are then asked what an elephant is. The first man touched its side and described the elephant as a wall. The second touched the tusk and believed the elephant to be a spear. The third felt the trunk and thought the elephant to be a snake. The fourth encountered the knee and believed the elephant to be a like a tree. The fifth touched the ear and thought the elephant to be a fan. The sixth man felt the tail and knew the elephant must be like a rope. The six men then argued about what an elephant is. One of the morals of this parable is the problem of looking at parts rather than the whole.

We feel the parable of the blind men and the elephant fits public relations. People often see bits and pieces of public relations through mass media filters. Some see it as a way for corporations to dupe stakeholders, some as words over substance, some as a mechanism for activists to change society for the better, and some as a way to improve the health of a nation. The truth is that public relations can be all of these. We defined public relations as the management of mutually-influential relationships within a web of stakeholder and organizational relationships. The outcome will not always be positive for stakeholders or even society. Corporations still have the most power and the exercise of that power can harm stakeholders. But public relations can also benefit society.

The point is that public relations plays a valuable role in society. A society cannot function effectively if the various webs of stakeholder and organizational relationships are fractured. Yes, at times the relationships are damaged, sometimes purposefully and through public relations. However, the relationships can be repaired and public relations has a vital role in those repair efforts. Public relations is not perfect; but it is an overstatement to call it a "necessary evil" in society. Like all elements of society, it has its good points and its bad points. Public relations is a societal tool, and tools can be misused. People have used crowbars in robberies and murders. But that does not mean crowbars are inherently evil. Public relations provides valuable societal benefits; it helps to maintain the relationships necessary for the effective functioning of society.

References

About Bretton Woods Project (n.d.). Retrieved March 22, 2006 from http://www.brettonwoodsproject.org/project/index.shtml.

About public relations (2005). Retrieved September 17, 2005 from http://www.prsa.org/_Resources/Profession/index.asp?ident=prof1.

About us (n.d.). Retrieved March 22, 2006 from http://www.oxfam.org/en/about/.

Agle, B. R., Mitchell, R. K., and Sonnenfeld, J. A. (1999). Who matters to CEOs? An investigation of stakeholder attributes and salience, corporate performance, and CEO values. *Academy of Management Journal, 42*: 507–25.

Alinsky, S. D. (1971). *Rules for Radicals: A Pragmatic Primer for Realistic Radicals.* New York: Random House.

Alsop, R. J. (2004). *The 18 Immutable Laws of Corporate Reputation: Creating, Protecting, and Repairing Your Most Valuable Asset.* New York: Free Press.

AMA war chest (1948, December 18). *Time, 52*: p. 44.

Angell, M. (2004). *The Truth about the Drug Companies: How They Deceive Us and What To Do About It.* New York: Random House.

Anti-Slavery Society (2005). Retrieved August 6, 2005 from http://www.spartacus.schoolnet.co.uk/USAantislavery.htm.

Arnold, C. A. (1989). Beyond self-interest: Policy entrepreneurs and aid to the homeless. *Policy Studies Journal, 18*: 47–66.

Aziz, S. (1993). Countries must play to win. *The Banker, 143*: 12–13.

—— (2004, March). Betting on buzz. *Pharmaceutical Executive, 24*: 118–20.

Bentele, G. (2005). Public sphere (Öffentlickeit). In R. L. Heath (ed.), *Encyclopedia of Public Relations* (vol. 2, pp. 706–10). Thousand Oaks, CA: Sage.

Bishop, R. L. (1988). What newspapers say about public relations. *Public Relations Review, 14*: 50—2.

Botan. C., and Taylor, M. (2004). Public relations: The state of the field. *Journal of Communications, 54(4)*: 645–61.

References

Bourdieu, P. (1985). The forms of capital. In J. G. Richardson (ed.), *Handbook of Theory and Research for the Sociology of Education* (pp. 241–58). New York: Greenwood.

Bowen, S. (2005a). Ethics of public relations. In R. L. Heath (ed.), *Encyclopedia of Public Relations* (vol. 1, pp. 294–7). Thousand Oaks, CA: Sage.

—— (2005b). Excellence theory. In R. L. Heath (ed.), *Encyclopedia of Public Relations* (vol. 1, pp. 306–8). Thousand Oaks, CA: Sage.

—— (2005c). Symmetry. In R. L. Heath (ed.), *Encyclopedia of Public Relations* (vol. 2, pp. 837—9). Thousand Oaks, CA: Sage.

Bronn, P. (2001). Communication managers as strategists? Can they make the grade? *Journal of Communications Management, 5*: 313–26.

Bryson, J. M. (2004). What to do when stakeholders matter: Stakeholder identification analysis techniques. *Public Management Review, 6*: 21–53.

Buckley, F. (2004, April 7). No smiles for Wal-Mart in California. Retrieved March 5, 2006 from http://money.cnn.com/2004/04/07/news/fortune500/walmart_inglewood.

Burrell, G. (1996). Normal science, paradigms, metaphors, discourses and genealogies of analysis. In S. Clegg, C. Hardy, and W. Nord (eds.), *Handbook of Organizational Studies* (pp. 642–58). London: Sage.

Burrow, J. G. (1963). *AMA: Voice of American Medicine*. Baltimore: Johns Hopkins University Press.

Canan, P. (1989). The SLAPP from a sociological perspective. *Sociological Review, 7*: 23–32.

Canan, P. and Pring, G. W. (1988). Strategic lawsuits against public participation. *Social Problems, 35*: 506–19.

Carroll, A. (1999). Corporate social responsibility. *Business and Society, 38(4)*: 268–96.

Carry A. Nation: "The famous and original bar room smasher" curriculum packet (2001). Retrieved August 6, 2005 from http://www.kshs.org/exhibits/carry/carry.pdf.

Chase, W. H. (1977). Public issue management: The new science. *Public Relations Journal, 33(10)*: 25–6.

—— (1980, Spring). Issues and policy. *Public Relations Quarterly, 25*: 5–6.

Coombs, W. T. (1993). Philosophical underpinnings: Ramifications of a pluralist paradigm. *Public Relations Review, 19*: 111–20.

—— (1998). The Internet as potential equalizer: New leverage for confronting social irresponsibility. *Public Relations Review, 24*: 289–304.

—— (2002). Assessing online issue threats: Issue contagions and their effect on issue prioritization. *Journal of Public Affairs, 2*: 215–29.

Cooper, R. (1997, Summer). A historical look at the PepsiCo/Burma boycott. *The Boycott Quarterly, 28*: 13–15.

References

Corporate Conscience Award (2003, October 8). Retrieved March 6, 2006 from http://www.chiquita.com/chiquita/announcements/releases/pr031008a.asp.

Crable, R. E. and Vibbert, S. L. (1985). Managing issues and influencing public policy. *Public Relations Review*, 11: 3–16.

Crusades (2005). Retrieved August 6, 2005 from http://www.wctu.com/crusades.html.

Cutlip, S. M. (1994). *The Unseen Power: Public Relations. A History.* Hillsdale, NJ: Lawrence Erlbaum Associates.

—— (1995). *Public Relations History: From the 17th to the 20th Century. The Antecedents.* Hillsdale, NJ: Lawrence Erlbaum Associates.

Cutlip, S. M., Center, A. H., and Broom, G. M. (1994). *Effective Public Relations*, 7th edn. Upper Saddle River, NJ: Prentice-Hall.

Davies, G., Chun, R., da Silva, R. V., and Roper, S. (2003). *Corporate Reputation and Competitiveness.* New York: Routledge.

Deibel, T. and Roberts, W. (1976). *Culture and Information: Two Foreign Policy Functions.* Newbury Park, CA: Sage.

Dezenhall, E. (2004). Who we are manifesto. Retrieved August 10, 2005 from http://www.dezenhall.com/about_manifesto.htm.

—— (2005). Stopping the attackers in today's assault culture. Retrieved August 8, 2005 from http://www.prwatch.org/documents/nichols-dezenhall.pdf.

Donkin, R. (1997, September 8). A moral stance: Companies can no longer shrug off the ethical aspects of their business. *Financial Times*, p. 16.

Dowling, G. (2002). *Creating Corporate Reputations: Identity, Image, and Performance.* New York: Oxford University Press.

Echoes from the triangle fire, *The Ladies' Garment Worker.* Retrieved March 7, 2006 from http://www.ilr.cornell.edu/trianglefire/texts/newsppaer/lgw_0911.html.

Ecuador rejects EU banana tariff proposal (2005, September 13). Retrieved September 16, 2005 from http://news.yahoo.com/news?tmpl=story&u=/nm/20050913/wl_nm/economy_ecuador_bananas_dc.

Emergency preparedness (2006). Retrieved February 17, 2006 from http://www.adcouncil.org/default.aspx?id=50.

Episode 106: Ali and the Valli Girls (2005). Retrieved August 10, 2005 from http://www.mtv.com/onair/dyn/power_girls/episode.jhtml?episodeID=86189.

Ewen, S. (1996). *PR! A Social History of Spin.* New York: Basic Books.

Exploring the links between international business and poverty reduction (2005). Retrieved March 3, 2006 from http://www.oxfam.org.uk/what_we_do/issues/livelihoods/unilever.htm.

FedEx expands low emission vehicle program to New York (2004, October 20). Retrieved March 2, 2006 from http://home.businesswire.com/portal/site/fedex-corp/index.jsp?epi-content=GENERIC&newsId=20041020005264&ndm

References

Hsc=v2*A1072962000000*B1143423296000*C1104584399000*DgroupByDate*
J2*N1001689&newsLang=en&beanID=1296635262&viewID=news_view.

Fisher, W. R. (1970). A motive view of communication. *Quarterly Journal of Speech*, 56: 131–9.

Fombrun, C. J. and van Riel, C. B. M. (2004). *Fame and fortune: How Successful Companies Build Winning Reputations*. New York: Prentice-Hall/Financial Times.

Freeman, R. E. (1984). *Strategic Management: A Stakeholder Approach*. Marshfield, MA: Pittman.

Gandy, O. H., Jr. (1982). *Beyond Agenda Setting: Information Subsidies and Public Policy*. Norwood, NJ: Ablex Publishing.

GAO (2000). FDA oversight of direct-to-consumer advertising had limits. Retrieved February 17, 2006 from http://www.gao.gov/new.items/d03177. pdf#search='gao%20DTC%202000'.

General Information (2005). Retrieved August 6, 2005 from http://www.afa.net/.

Getting in gear (2005). Retrieved March 2, 2006 from http://ww.fedex.com/us/ about/responsibility/envrionment/hybridelectricvehicle.html?link=4.

Gilbert, M. (2005, March 10). 'PoweR girls' deliver bad PR. *Boston Globe*, p. B6.

Going global: Managers' experiences working with worldwide stakeholders (2005). Center for Corporate Citizenship. Retrieved September 9, 2005 from http://www.bcccc.net/index.cfm?fuseaction=Page.viewPage&pageId=1082& grandparentID=490&parentID=569.

Greider, W. (2003, July 31). Victory at McDonald's. *The Nation*, 277: 8–12.

Grunig, J. E. (1992). *Excellence in Public Relations and Communication Management*. Hillsdale, NJ: Lawrence Erlbaum Associates.

—— (2001). Two-way symmetrical public relations: Past, present, and future. In R. L. Heath (ed.), *Handbook of Public Relations* (pp. 11–30). Thousand Oaks, CA: Sage.

Grunig, J. E. and Hon, L. C. (1999). Guidelines for measuring relationships in public Relations. Retrieved March 25, 2005 from http://www.instituteforpr. comn/measeval/rel_p1.htm.

Grunig, J. E. and Hunt, T. (1984). *Managing Public Relations*. New York: Holt, Rinehart & Winston.

Grunig, J. E. and Repper, F. C. (1992). Strategic management, publics, and issues. In J. E. Grunig (ed.), *Excellence in Public Relations and Communication Management* (pp. 117–57). Hillsdale, NJ: Lawrence Erlbaum Associates.

Grunig, J. E. and White, J. (1992). The effect of worldviews on public relations theory and practice. In J. E. Grunig (ed.), *Excellence in Public Relations and Communication Management* (pp. 31–64). Hillsdale, NJ: Lawrence Erlbaum Associates.

Guidance: FDA's "drug watch" for emerging drug safety information (2005, May). Retrieved August 15, 2005 from http://www.fda.gov/cder/guidance/6657dft.pdf.

Hall, J. (2005, July 3). Dealing with terror: British companies have been chastised by Kate Hoey, the Labour MP, for not doing enough to ensure that they are not giving financial succour to Zimbabwe's repressive regime. *Sunday Telegraph*, p. 3.

Harris, R. (1969). *A Sacred Trust*. Baltimore: Penguin.

Hazleton, V. and Kennan, W. (2000). Social capital: Reconceptualizing the bottom line. *Corporate Communication, 5(2)*: 81–6.

Heath, R. L. (1997). *Strategic Issues Management: Organizations and Public Policy Challenges*. Thousand Oaks, CA: Sage.

—— (1998). New communication technologies: An issues management point of view. *Public Relations Review, 24*: 273–88.

—— (2001). A rhetorical enactment rationale for public relations: The good organization communicating well. In R. L. Heath (ed.), *Handbook of Public Relations* (pp. 31–50). Thousand Oaks, CA: Sage.

—— (2005). Mutually beneficial relations. In R. L. Heath (ed.), *Encyclopedia of Public Relations* (vol. 2, pp. 552–6). Thousand Oaks, CA: Sage.

Heath, R. L. and Coombs, W. T. (2006). *Today's Public Relations: An Introduction*. Thousands Oaks, CA: Sage.

Heath, R. L. and Nelson, R. A. (1986). *Issues Management*. Beverly Hills, CA: Sage.

Henderson, J. K. (1998). Negative connotations in the use of the term "public relations" in the print media. *Public Relations Review, 22*: 45–54.

Hitler, A. (1998) [1925]. *Mein Kampf*. Mariner Books.

Hitler's anti-tobacco campaign (2005). Retrieved August 2, 2005 from http://constitutionalistnc.tripod.com/hitlerleftist/id1.html.

Hoffman, A. J. and Ocasio, W. (2001). Not all events are attended equally: Toward a middle-range theory of industry attention to external events. *Organization Science, 12*: 414–34.

Holtzhausen, D. R. (2000). Postmodern values in public relations. *Journal of Public Relations Research, 12*: 93–114.

Holtzhausen, D. R. and Voto, R. (2002). Resistance from the margins: The postmodern public relations practitioner as organizational activist. *Journal of Public Relations Research, 14*: 57–84.

Horton, J. (2005). Ethics anyone? Retrieved September 17, 2005 from http://online-pr.blogspot.com/2005/01/ethicsanyone.html.

"I will be heard": Abolitionism in America. (2005). Retrieved August 6, 2005 from http://rmc.library.cornell.edu/abolitionism/.

International Association of Business Communicators Code of Ethics for Professional Communicators. Available: http://www.iabc.com/members/joining/code.htm.

Iritani, E. (2005, February 20). From the street to the inner sanctum. *Los Angeles Times*, p. C-1.

IRN (n.d.). Retrieved March, 22, 2006 from http://www.irn.org/basics/ard/index.php?id=/basics/about.html.

Irvine, R. A. (2004, January). How to succeed like an activist in 2004: 9 suggestions for corporate PR folks. Retrieved August 10, 2005 from http://www.epublicrelations.ca/.

Iwata, E. and Patrick, D. (2004, December 15). Jones sues BALCO founder, denies steroid use. *USA Today*, p. 10C.

Jones, B. L. and Chase, W. H. (1979). Managing public policy issues. *Public Relations Review*, 7: 3–23.

Keck, M . E. and Sikkink, K. (1998). *Activists Beyond Borders: Advocacy Networks in International Politics*. Ithaca, NY: Cornell University Press.

Keenan, K. L. (1996, July). Coverage of public relations on network television news: An exploratory census of content. Paper presented to the Association for Education in Journalism, Anaheim, CA.

Key, V. O., Jr. (1964). *Politics, Parties, and Pressure Groups*. New York: Thomas Y. Crowell.

Kingdon, J. W. (1984). *Agendas, Alternatives, and Public Policies*. Boston: Little, Brown.

Kosicki, G. M. (1993). Problems and opportunities in agenda-setting research. *Journal of Communication*, 43(2): 100–27.

Kunczik, M. (1990). *Images of Nations and International Public Relations*. Bonn: Friedrich-Ebert-Stiftung.

—— (1994, June). Public diplomacy and public relations advertisements of foreign countries in Germany: Results of a content analysis. Paper presented at the annual meeting of the International Communication Association, Sydney, Australia.

Laermer, R. (2004). *Full Frontal PR: Building Buzz about Your Business, Your Product, or You*. Princeton, NJ: Bloomberg Press.

Leitch, S. and Neilson, D. (2001). Bring publics into public relations: New theoretical frameworks for practice. In R. L. Heath (ed.), *Handbook of Public Relations* (pp. 127–38). Thousand Oaks, CA: Sage.

Lennick, D. and Kiel, F. (2005). *Moral Intelligence: Enhancing Business Performance and Leadership Success*. Upper Saddle River, NJ: Wharton School Publishing.

L'Etang, J. (1996). Public relations as diplomacy. In J. L'Etang and M. Pieczka (eds.), *Critical Perspectives in Public Relations* (pp. 14–34). London: International Thomson Business Press.

References

Lewis, C. (2003). The impact of direct-to-consumer advertising. Retrieved August 15, 2005 from http://www.fda.gov/fdac/features/2003/203_dtc.html.

Lewis, S. (2003, January). Reputation and corporate responsibility. Retrieved March 15, 2004 from http://www.mori.com/publications/sl/reputation-and-csr.pdf.

Lin, N. (1999). Building a network theory of social capital. *Connections, 22*: 28–51.

Lucas, G. (2004, April 4). A Wal-mart in the neighborhood? Inglewood goes to polls to decide. *San Francisco Chronicle*, p. A-1.

Manheim, J. B. (1987). A model of agenda dynamics. In M. L. McLaughlin (ed.), *Communication Yearbook 10* (pp. 499–516). New York: Sage.

—— (1991). *All the People, All the Time: Strategic Public Communication and American Politics.* New York: M. E. Sharpe.

—— (1994). *Strategic Public Diplomacy and America Foreign Policy: The Evolution of Influence.* New York: Oxford University Press.

—— (2001). *The Death of a Thousand Cuts: Corporate Campaigns and the Attacks on the Corporation.* Mahwah, NJ: Lawrence Erlbaum Associates.

Marlowe, L. (1998, December 10). Amnesty and Body Shop put their mark on human rights. *The Irish Times*, p. 12.

McGinn, D. (2005, November 14). Wal-Mart hits the wall. Retrieved February 13, 2006 from http://www.msnbc.msn.com/id/7279844/did/9938407/site/newsweek.

McGuire, W. J. (1981). Theoretical foundations of campaigns. In R. E. Rice and W. J. Paisley (eds.), *Public Communication Campaigns* (pp. 41–70). Beverly Hills: Sage.

Mintzes, B., Barer, M. L., Kravitz, R. L., Kazanjian, A., Bassett, K., Lexchin, J., Evans, R. G., Pan, R., and Marion, S. A. (2005, February 2). Influence of direct to consumer pharmaceutical advertising and patients' requests on prescribing: Two site cross sectional survey. *British Medical Journal, 324*: 278–9.

Mitchell, R. K., Agle, B. R., and Wood, D. J. (1997). Toward a theory of stakeholder identification and salience: Defining the principles of who and what really counts. *Academy of Management Review, 22*: 853–86.

Moynihan, R. and Cassels, A. (2005). *Selling Sickness: How the World's Biggest Pharmaceutical Companies are Turning Us All into Patients.* New York: National Books.

Moynihan, R., Heath, I., and Henry, D. (2002, April 13). Selling sickness: The pharmaceutical industry and disease mongering. *British Medical Journal, 324*: 886–90.

Muckraking (2005). Retrieved August 6, 2005 from http://www.spartacus.schoolnet.co.uk/Jmuckraking.htm.

Mumby, D. (1988). *Communication and Power in Organizations: Discourse, Ideology and Domination.* Norwood, NJ: Ablex Publishing.

Murphy, P. and Dee, J. (1992). Reconciling the preferences of environmental activists and corporate policymakers. *Journal of Public Relations Research*, 8: 1–34.

Negin, E. (1996, September/October). The alar "scare" was real; and so is the "veggie hate" movement. *Columbia Journalism Review*, 35: 13–15.

Neuman, J. (1996). *Lights, Camera, War: Is Media Technology Driving International Politics?* New York: St Martin's Press.

Newsom, D., Turk, J. V., and Kruckeberg, D. (2004). *This is PR: The Realities of Public Relations*, 8th edn. Belmont, CA: Wadsworth.

Ocasio, W. (1997). Towards an attention-based view of the firm. *Strategic Management Journal*, 18: 187–206.

Our mission (n.d.). Retrieved March 22, 2006 from http://www.sfcg.org/sfcg/sfcg_mission.html.

Paletz, D. L. and Entman, R. M. (1981). *Media Power Politics*. New York: Free Press.

Parents' Internet monitoring study (2005). Retrieved February 17, 2005 from http://www.netsmartz.org/safety/statistics.htm.

Paul, J. A. (2000, June). NGOs and global policy-making. Retrieved September 21, 2005 from http://globalpolicy.igc.org/ngos/analysis/anal100,thm.

Pell, E. (1990, March/April). No sacred cows. *Common Cause Magazine*, 10: 6–7.

People & Events: 1857–1944 (2000). Retrieved August 6, 2005 from http://www.pbs.org/wgbh/amex/rockefellers/peopleevents/p_tarbell.html.

Pfizer Statement on PhRMA Principles (2005, August 2). Retrieved August 10, 2005 from http://www.Pfizer.com/Pfizer/are/news_release/2005pr/mn_2005_0802c.jsp.

PhRMA Guiding Principles: Direct to consumer advertisements about prescription medicines (2005, August). Retrieved August 10, 2005 from http://www.phrma.org/publications/policy/2005-08-02.1194.pdf#search='PhRMA %20guiding%20principles.

Pollution: Keep America beautiful – Iron Eyes Cody (1961–1983) (2005). Retrieved August 10, 2005 from http://www.adcouncil.org/campaigns/historic_campaigns_pollution/.

PR Watch (2005). Retrieved August 5, 2005 from http://www.prwatch.org/prwissues.

PRSA Member Code of Ethics (2000). New York: Public Relations Society of America.

Putnam, R. D. (2000). *Bowling Alone: The Collapse and Revival of American Community*. New York: Simon & Schuster.

Rakow, L. F. (1989). Information and power: Toward a critical theory of information campaigns. In C. T. Salmon (ed.), *Information Campaigns: Balancing Social Values and Social Change* (pp. 164–84). Newbury Park, CA: Sage.

Raucher, A. R. (1968). *Public Relations and Business: 1900–1929*. Baltimore: Johns Hopkins University Press.

Rawlins, B. L. (2005). Corporate social responsibility. In R. L. Heath (ed.), *Encyclopedia of Public Relations* (vol. 1, pp. 210–14). Thousand Oaks, CA: Sage.

Reports of blindness in men using Viagra, Cialis (2005, May 27). Retrieved May 28, 2005 from http://www.msnbc.msn.com/id/8004291/print/1/displaymode/1098.

Ries, A. and Reis, L. (2002). *The Fall of Advertising and the Rise of PR*. New York: HarperCollins.

Roddick, A. (1996, October 31). Body Shop challenges Shell to confront "new business reality." *Financial Times*, p. 14.

Ryan, C. (1991). *Prime Time Activism: Media Strategies for Grass Roots Organizing*. Boston: South End Press.

Saxton, G. D. and Benson, M. A. (2005). Social capital and the growth of the nonprofit sector. *Social Science Quarterly, 86(1)*: 16–35.

Scheinderman, G. (2005). Temperance: Strategies and rights used. Retrieved from http://www.albany.edu/~gs8053/temperance.html.

Schultz, D. E. (2003). Evolving marketing and marketing communication into the twenty-first century. In D. Iacobucci and B. Calder (eds.), *Kellogg on Integrated Marketing* (pp. vii–xxi). Hoboken, NJ: John Wiley & Sons.

Scrimger, J. and Richards, T. (2003). Public relations battles and wars: Journalistic clichés and the potential for conflict resolution. *Public Relations Review, 29*: 485–92.

Sheehan, K. B. (2003). Balancing acts: An analysis of Food and Drug Administration letters about direct-to-consumer advertising violations. *Journal of Public Policy & Marketing, 22*: 159–69.

Signitzer, B. H. and Coombs, T. (1992). Public relations and public diplomacy: Conceptual convergences. *Public Relations Review, 18(2)*: 137–47.

Simola, S. (2003). Ethics of justice and care in corporate crisis management. *Journal of Business Ethics, 46*: 351–61.

Sofer, S. (1991). Debate revisited: Practice over theory. In W. C. Olsen (ed.), *The Theory and Practice of International Relations*, 8th edn. (pp. 65–77). Englewood Cliffs, NJ: Prentice-Hall.

Spicer, C. H. (1993). Images of public relations in print media. *Journal of Public Relations Research, 5*: 47–61.

Stadler, J. (n.d.). Online child molesters. Retrieved February 17, 2006 from http://www.netsmartz.org/news/onlinemolesters.htm.

Starck, K. and Kruckeberg, D. (2003). Ethical obligations of public relations in an era of globalisation. *Journal of Communication Management, 8(1)*: 29–40.

Starr, P. (1982). *The Social Transformation of American Medicine*. New York: Basic Books.

Stauber, J. and Rampton, S. (1995). *Toxic Sludge is Good for You! Lies, Damn Lies and the Public Relations Industry*. Monroe, ME: Common Courage Press.

References

Taylor, M. (2005). Nongovernmental organizations (NGOs). In R. L. Heath (ed.), *Encyclopedia of Public Relations* (vol. 2, pp. 576–8). Thousand Oaks, CA: Sage.

Tell Shell (2005). Tell Shell forum. Retrieved October 1, 2005 from http://www.tellshellforum.shell.com/startFrame.aspx?messageID=25.

To serve and to preserve: Improving public administration in a competitive world (2000). Asian Development Bank. Retrieved March 25, 2006 from http://www.adb.org/Documents/Manuals/Serve_and_Preserve/

Treadwell, D. and Treadwell, J. B. (2005). *Public Relations Writing: Principles and Practice*, 2nd edn. Thousand Oaks, CA: Sage.

Ulmer, R. R., Seeger, M. W., and Sellnow, T. L. (2005). Stakeholder theory. In R. L. Heath (ed.), *Encyclopedia of Public Relations* (vol. 2, pp. 808–11). Thousand Oaks, CA: Sage.

Upton Sinclair (2005). Retrieved August 6, 2005 from http://www.spartacus.schoolnet.co.uk/Jupton.htm.

van Riel, C. B. M. (2000). Corporate communication orchestrated by a sustainable story. In M. Schultz, M. J. Hatch, and M. H. Larsen (eds.), *The Expressive Organization: Linking Identity, Reputation, and the Corporate Brand* (pp. 157–81). New York: Oxford University Press.

Vasquez, G. M. and Taylor, M. (2001). Research perspectives on "the public." In R. L. Heath (ed.), *Handbook of Public Relations* (pp. 139–54). Thousand Oaks, CA: Sage.

Weelwright, J. (2001, August 19). Interview: Anita Roddick. *Scotland on Sunday*, p. 8.

What is civil society? Retrieved February 12, 2006 from http://www.fao.org/tc/NGO/index_en.asp.

Wilcox, D., Ault, P. H., Agee, W. K., and Cameron, G. T. (2000). *Essentials of Public Relations*. Boston: Allyn & Bacon.

Witte, K., Meyer, G., and Martell, D. (2001). *Effective Health Risk Messages: A Step-by-Step Guide*. Thousand Oaks, CA: Sage.

Wyeth support PhRMA guiding principles for direct-to-consumer advertising (2005, August 2). Retrieved August 5, 2005 from http://www.wyeth.com/news/Pressed_and_released/pr08_02_2005_15_43_03.asp.

Index